This book is from

the kitchen library of

_____

_____

Mr. Food®

FROM
MY
KITCHEN TO
YOURS

Stories and Recipes from Home

Art Ginsburg
Mr. Food®

WILLIAM MORROW AND COMPANY, INC.

NEW YORK

Library of Congress Cataloging-in-Publication Data

Ginsburg, Art.
    Mr. Food®, from my kitchen to yours : stories and recipes from home / Art Ginsburg.
      p. cm.
    ISBN 0-688-14512-4 (hardcover)
    1. Cookery.   I. Title.
  TX714.G573   1996
  641.5—DC20   96-26799
                                        CIP

Printed in the United States of America

First Edition

  2   3   4   5   6   7   8   9   10

BOOK DESIGN AND ELECTRONIC PAGE MAKEUP BY MICHAEL MENDELSOHN OF MM DESIGN 2000, INC.

From my early years,
I have been fortunate to have never been in want of food.

This book is dedicated to those at
Second Harvest® Food Banks all around this country,
who help keep millions of Americans (mostly children)
from going hungry.

By following their lead and doing our part
to feed the hungry, together we can all look forward
to eliminating hunger and sharing in the

"OOH IT'S SO GOOD!!®"

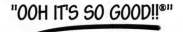

Once again, the team at **Mr. Food**® certainly made it all click.

Steve   Chuck   Caryl   Howard   Tom

Acknowledgments

This has to be one of my most exciting books yet. Why? Because it's given me the opportunity to share a part of me that most of you have never seen before. I think you'll especially like the photos I've included. We haven't used photos in my previous books, but you'll see that they really helped this book **develop**. And like the parts of a puzzle, these photographs really helped me chronicle the many stages of my life. And, once again, the team at **Mr. Food**® certainly made it all **click**. None of this would have been possible without the **focus** of Caryl Ginsburg Fantel and Howard Rosenthal. They helped me see the big **picture** and keep everything **clear**. And as Mom and Dad were, Ethel, Flo, Steve, Chuck, Carol, Roy, Tammy, and my grandchildren continue to be the **light source** that shines upon me every day.

The stories in this book have reminded me and my family of so many wonderful times, and so, too, have the foods. Making all these unforgettable foods was a unique task, since my recipe testing staff had to help re-create specific tastes and textures, mostly with just our memories to guide them. I owe a great deal to Joe, Patty, Janice, Cheryl, and Jo Ann for their patience and perseverance as Ethel, the kids, and I each took turns describing our own memories of these foods. After they perfected each dish, Laura artfully took **aim** to make sure the recipe directions were up to **speed**. I'm also thankful for the support of the rest of my incredible staff: Marilyn, Beth, Chet, Tom, and Helayne.

Fortunately, Al, Zach, Deborah, Richard, Michael, Jackie, Kim, Anne, and all my friends at William Morrow are always there to keep each **frame** moving along smoothly. Bill Adler, Michael Mendelsohn, and Phil Scheuer sure do make it all come together in a **snap**.

Once again, it's the many supportive food companies and associations, especially those below, as well as my enthusiastic viewers and readers, who give me the best reasons to happily **pose** for each photo, so that I can capture all the moments full of "OOH IT'S SO GOOD!!®"

Campbell Soup Company

The Coca-Cola Company

Doug DeLisle, *The Record,* Troy, New York

Best Foods, a Division of CPC International Inc.

Joe's Stone Crab Restaurant

Kahlúa Liqueur

Kellogg's®

Mars, Incorporated

McIlhenny Company

The National Turkey Federation

Nestlé Beverage Company

Rascal House Restaurant

Sunkist®

Thomas J. Lipton Company

The Vanilla Bean Baking Co.

Variety Club Tent 7

Villa Valenti Restaurant

My thanks to all my generous fans who have shared their personal photographs with me throughout the years.

Contents

Recipe Contents

Appetizers

Soups, Salads, Sauces, and Dressings

Chicken and Turkey

Fish and Seafood

Pasta

Side Dishes

Desserts

Hodgepodge

I've had this passion for food ever since I was a kid growing up in Troy, New York.

Introduction

My wife was right . . . I have to admit it. She always said that I have a story for everything. And it's always been the truth, especially when it comes to food!

Well, why not? We all eat. It's just that some of us get into it more than others. Like me! I want to do more than eat simply to satisfy my hunger. I want to know all I can about different foods, 'cause then I enjoy them even more, while taking away a memory or two to satisfy my appetite for life.

Thinking about it, I'd have to say that I've had this passion for food ever since I was a kid growing up in Troy, New York. And, since then, I've been fortunate to meet so many interesting people and travel to so many wonderful places—along the way, being exposed to a world of different food tastes, textures, and aromas. And I've found that, later on, those tastes and smells have triggered memories that let me relive my adventures again and again!

Besides all the wonderful experiences I've had since the birth of **Mr. Food**® in 1971, I feel fortunate to have had a rich family background that has helped me experience the full tastes of life. And now I finally get a chance to share some of my favorite memories with *you*. Of course, they're wrapped up with the recipes that are closest to my heart, too.

People often ask me how I got interested in food or where I was trained. Since I spent a good part of my childhood in my father's butcher shop in the 1930s and '40s, I learned how to handle a knife at a pretty early age. I also learned lots more than I wanted to know at the time about all kinds of meat and poultry. I'm glad now, but oh, those freezing cold early mornings spent plucking chicken feathers left their impression on me!

In those days I worked hard with Dad, and I played hard, too.

My kids still can't believe my stories of how, after playing in my high school football games, I'd go out for a bite with the guys. I'd usually order lasagna. But while I was waiting for it to cook, I'd down a hot meatball sandwich *and* a whole pizza! After all, I was a growing boy!

I've mentioned my mom, Jennie, in previous books, telling what a good cook she was. Actually, what made her food so special was that she was creative . . . she *had* to be. My dad often went out into the country to buy cattle from local farmers. If they had extra produce, Dad would come home with a bushel basket full of cauliflower or maybe cabbage, peppers, or corn. So Mom had to find loads of different ways to prepare whatever Dad brought home. I guess that's where my adventurous food spirit was born—I learned that I'd have to taste anything she served, even if I didn't think I was going to like it. Of course, I usually *did* like whatever it was she made!

And when I got married, I realized that our kitchen was missing something crucial . . . Mom! We kid my wife, Ethel, about how, when we got married, she couldn't even boil water. Oh, but she took to the kitchen in no time! Mom and my sister, Flo, taught her their secrets, and by the time our three kids came along, our house was the place where all the neighborhood kids came for great meals and goodies. In fact, as Ethel and I started our own catering business, the five of us became the family who cooked together.

The kids were always with us as we grew that business. They went along to all our parties, so they had no choice but to work by our sides. It sure kept them safe and taught them a thing or two about hard work. And even though Ethel and I worked like crazy in those days, we all had lots of fun, too. Even now, when one of us tells any one of hundreds of truly unbelievable stories from our catering days, it gets the rest of us laughing so hard that we keep going and going!

Ginsburg Caterers had a reputation for serving tasty, real homemade food with a gourmet look—and I made sure we never ran out of anything at our parties. I never wanted to have to tell someone who wanted more of something, "I'm sorry, but there's no more"—and I never did. Oh, the food we made . . . ! This book has given us the opportunity to share a load of catering recipes that we kept secret for years, even though we got interesting offers to reveal them!

I've also dusted off some pictures from my early acting days. While we were busy catering, I'd take whatever time I could and pursue my other love . . . acting. It's a good thing I did, 'cause that's what got me started as **Mr. Food**®!

When you read about when I first put on my **Mr. Food**® chef's hat and pocketed white apron, you'll see how I got to combine my loves—food, people, and performing. You'll see some of the places I've been and the people I've met and, of course, the recipes I've collected along the way.

And in addition to those recipes, I've got recipes that, when first introduced, used new food products that were being popularized all over the country—like the famous Campbell's Tomato Soup–Spice Cake (page 31) and Lipton® California Onion Dip (page 88), which we all made with that "new onion soup mix" in the 1950s—and recipes from famous and not-so-famous restaurants from all over the country that I love (and frequent)!

After you read about my childhood, my navy antics, my family, my years as a caterer, and some of my favorite **Mr. Food**® experiences, I think you'll understand why I love food and love what I do so much. I've done something new with this book, and I hope you like it! I just wish I had had the room to tell even more tales—maybe someday soon I'll be able to share even more recipes and stories from home. After all, every day, every meal is an adventure. So, sit back and get ready to find out where all the *"OOH IT'S SO GOOD!!®"* comes from. Then you'll be set to cook up your own stories and recipes from home.

A Note About Packaged Foods

Packaged food sizes may vary by brand. Generally, the sizes indicated in these recipes are average sizes. If you can't find the exact package size listed in the ingredients, whatever package is closest in size will usually do the trick.

I generally don't mention specific brands in my recipes. But in this book I sometimes do, since certain recipes that I (and many of us) grew up with were created by food companies with their specific products in mind. These companies have been most cooperative in providing historical background to help in the re-creation of many of my fondest food memories.

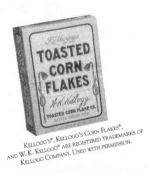

KELLOGG'S®, KELLOGG'S CORN FLAKES®, AND W. K. KELLOGG® ARE REGISTERED TRADEMARKS OF KELLOGG COMPANY. USED WITH PERMISSION.

PHOTOGRAPH COURTESY OF BEST FOODS, A DIVISION OF CPC INTERNATIONAL INC.

"M&M's"® CHOCOLATE CANDIES, CIRCA 1940 - 1950. "M&M's"® CHOCOLATE CANDIES IS A REGISTERED TRADEMARK OF MARS, INCORPORATED.

PHOTOGRAPH COURTESY OF CAMPBELL SOUP COMPANY

xx

A NESTLÉ® QUIK® CAN FROM THE EARLY 1960S. PHOTOGRAPH COURTESY OF THE NESTLÉ BEVERAGE COMPANY.

Mr. Food®

FROM

MY

KITCHEN TO

YOURS

GROWING UP
IN TROY

1

Here are Mom, Dad, and my sister, Flo, with the rest of Mom's family shortly before I was born.

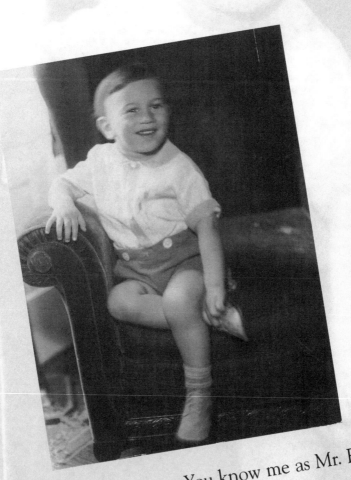

Well, here I am. You know me as Mr. Food, but in the early days I was known mostly as Art Ginsburg, or even as "Artie" or "Ginsy." Oh, what a beautiful baby I was!

Other than this one baby portrait, the earliest photo we have of me was taken when I was about 10 years old. That's because my family couldn't afford a camera in those early days. And even if we could have, we wouldn't have been able to afford the film and the processing. Fortunately, times have changed.

Here are Mom, Dad, and my sister, Flo (from the photo on pages 2–3 with the rest of Mom's family) shortly before I was born. Boy, did I ever add excitement to the family. And, judging from the looks on most of their faces, they needed it!

Since I wasn't exactly an angel of a child, I did get blamed for a lot of things, even when I *wasn't* guilty. Sure, I was born during the Depression, but when my sister blamed me for *that,* she went a bit too far!

As far back as I can remember, on Friday nights Mom would light the Sabbath candles, Dad would say the blessings over the wine and challah, and then we'd all enjoy a traditional meal together.

Often when I was propped up in my wooden high chair, Mom would cut some of her fresh, soft matzo balls (that came out perfectly every time with Aunt Sarah's recipe) into tiny pieces and serve them to me with a little cup of her long-cooked chicken soup (lukewarm, of course). Mom was famous for her chicken soup. Sometimes she'd serve it plain, sometimes with rice, noodles, or matzo balls. But the one thing we could always count on was that it would be served with lots of love.

Homemade Chicken Soup

6 to 8 servings

One 2½- to 3-pound chicken, cut into 8 pieces
10 cups cold water
4 carrots, peeled and cut into 1-inch chunks
3 celery stalks, cut into 1-inch chunks

2 medium-sized onions, cut into 1-inch chunks
1 tablespoon salt
1½ teaspoons black pepper

Combine all the ingredients in a soup pot and bring to a boil over high heat. Reduce the heat to low, then simmer for 2½ to 3 hours, or until the chicken easily falls off the bones. Serve the soup with the chicken (bones and all) or, if desired, use tongs to remove the chicken from the soup and allow the chicken to cool slightly. Then bone and skin the chicken, cut it into small pieces, and return it to the soup. Serve as is or with noodles, rice, or matzo balls (see Note).

NOTE: Store any leftover soup in the refrigerator. Before reheating, remove and discard any fat that has risen to the surface. For homemade matzo ball soup, prepare matzo balls (page 7) and add them to the soup pot about 15 minutes before serving. For chicken noodle soup, add ¼ pound medium egg noodles, cooked, to the soup just before serving, and for chicken rice soup, add 3 cups cooked rice.

Aunt Sarah's Matzo Balls

about 1 dozen matzo balls

4 eggs
½ cup water
⅓ cup vegetable shortening,
    melted

1 teaspoon salt
1 cup matzo meal

In a large bowl, combine the eggs, water, shortening, and salt; mix well. Add the matzo meal and stir until combined; do not overmix. Cover and chill for 30 minutes. Remove the matzo ball mixture from the refrigerator; wet your hands slightly, and form the mixture into 1-inch balls. Meanwhile, bring a large pot of water to a rolling boil over medium-high heat. Carefully drop the balls into the boiling water; cover and cook for 20 minutes, or until the matzo balls float to the top and are completely cooked inside. Remove the matzo balls with a slotted spoon and place in a shallow baking dish; cover and chill until ready to reheat in a pot of chicken soup. Or, to serve immediately, remove the matzo balls from their cooking pot and add to a pot of hot chicken soup.

When I was a little guy, it seemed like all my mom did from sunrise to sunset was take care of Flo and me, and cook. We had a kosher home, so even if there had been convenience foods as there are today, Mom probably wouldn't have paid attention to most of them.

When Mom took us for a walk, down First Street we'd go, then on to Congress Street, and, eventually, back home. Sometimes she'd buy a fresh challah at the bakery, and it was my job to carry it back home without crushing it. But when Mom had time, she'd bake her own challah. It was always better than store-bought, or at least that's what I thought back then, 'cause I liked watching her make and braid the dough, and I loved the way the whole house smelled while it was baking. That's an aroma you never forget. Sometimes there's no substitute for the real thing. Why not give this timeless favorite bread a try?

BREADS

Challah Bread

2 loaves

5 cups all-purpose flour, divided,
    plus more if needed
2 packages (¼ ounce each) active
    dry yeast
2 tablespoons sugar
1½ teaspoons salt
1 cup plus 1 tablespoon water,
    divided

⅓ cup butter
4 eggs
Nonstick vegetable spray
1 egg white
2 teaspoons poppy seeds (optional)

Preheat the oven to 400°F. In a large bowl, combine 2 cups flour, the yeast, sugar, and salt; set aside. In a small saucepan, heat 1 cup water and the butter over medium heat until the butter is melted, stirring occasionally. Pour over the flour mixture. Add the eggs and blend with an electric beater on medium speed for about 3 minutes, until moistened. With a spoon, stir in 2½ cups flour and mix until the dough pulls cleanly away from the sides of the bowl, adding more flour as needed. Place the dough on a lightly floured surface, knead in ½ cup flour, and continue kneading until the dough is smooth, about 3 to 5 minutes, adding more flour as needed. Place the dough in a large bowl that has been coated with nonstick vegetable spray. Spray the top of the dough with nonstick spray. Cover with plastic wrap, then a towel. Let rise at room temperature for 35 to 40 minutes, or until doubled in size. Punch down and divide in half. With your hands, stretch each piece of dough into a rectangle about 6" × 14". With a knife, make 2 cuts down the length of each piece of dough, starting 1 inch from one end and cutting through to the other end (see illustration 1). Braid the three strips of each piece of dough (see illustration 2) and tuck the ends underneath. Place each braided loaf on a rimmed baking sheet that has been coated with nonstick vegetable spray. Spray the dough with nonstick spray, cover loosely with plastic wrap, and let rise at room temperature for 20 to 25 minutes, or until doubled in size. Bake for 10 minutes. In a small bowl, combine the egg white and remaining 1 tablespoon water. Remove the bread from the oven and, with a pastry brush, brush the bread with the egg white mixture. If desired, sprinkle the tops with the poppy seeds. Return to the oven and bake for 5 to 10 more minutes, or until the loaves sound hollow when tapped with the handle of a flatware knife. Remove from the oven and cool on wire racks.

1.

2.

3.

Ever since I was a kid, I've loved spring! Sure, we all played in the snow all winter long, but after a few months of it, when our mountains of cold snow finally melted, we were aching to play ball and do other stuff outside again.

Springtime and the melting snow also meant that Dad would be bringing home fresh rhubarb from the farmers he dealt with. And, shortly after that, when the fresh strawberries were ready, it'd be time for Mom to combine rhubarb and strawberries into something with a most unusual taste and texture . . . she called it rhubarb and strawberry compote. Mom promised me that she'd used a whole load of sugar when she made it, but it still had a bite that made us pucker! (Sometimes Mom let me add sugar to my own so I wouldn't pucker so much.) Mom and Dad swore it was good for us, 'cause when they were young they ate it as a spring tonic. I don't know about that, but when *I* was young, I ate whatever they told me to eat. Now I look forward to this scrumptious treat.

When I was young,
I ate whatever they told me to eat.

Rhubarb and Strawberry Compote

4 to 6 servings

1 pound fresh rhubarb, trimmed
and cut into 1-inch pieces
(see Note)

1 cup sugar
2 cups fresh strawberries, hulled
and sliced

Place the rhubarb in a large bowl and add just enough cold water to cover; let stand for 10 minutes. Drain thoroughly and place in a medium-sized heavy saucepan. Sprinkle with the sugar and cook over low heat until the mixture begins to bubble. Cook for 5 more minutes, then add the strawberries. Cook for 15 to 20 minutes, slightly mashing the fruit with a fork as it cooks. Serve warm or cold.

NOTE: If it isn't fresh rhubarb season, you can substitute a 20-ounce package of frozen rhubarb for the fresh. (And you can even use a 16-ounce package of frozen whole strawberries, too.) Just thaw and drain them completely, then cook as directed above. This is great as is, but for a real treat, I like to use some chilled compote to top vanilla ice cream. It also makes a great topper for Challah French Toast (page 128).

As I've mentioned, my dad had a lot of contact with farmers. That's because he was a hardworking, old-fashioned type of butcher. And, before that, he was a cattle dealer. We say Dad was "from the old school." Unlike butchers of today, Dad did everything himself. He went directly to the cattle and poultry farmers to buy and slaughter the animals. He did all the trimming, plucking, and every other step involved in getting the meat to his customers.

One of the best parts of Dad's trade was that he'd bring home whatever meat cuts didn't sell. It was up to my mom to turn these leftover cuts into dinner for us. It was almost like a game to them—and Mom was so good at it! Take her Swiss steak—the taste was incredible! And the aroma of the simmering meat and onions was so tempting that it was enough to stir up appetites all around downtown Troy!

Jennie's Swiss Steak

4 to 6 servings

One 2-pound boneless beef chuck
steak, 1½ inches thick
4 large onions, cut into large
chunks

1 cup water
1 teaspoon salt
¾ teaspoon black pepper

In a large nonstick skillet or pot, brown the steak on one side for 4 to 5 minutes over medium-high heat. Turn the steak and place the onions around it; brown the steak on the second side for 4 to 5 minutes. Reduce the heat to medium and, using tongs, lift up the steak; stir the onions and place the steak over the onions. Continue cooking for 20 to 25 more minutes, until the onions begin to turn golden, lifting the steak and stirring occasionally. In a small bowl, combine the water, salt, and pepper. Pour over the steak and reduce the heat to low. Partially cover and simmer for 1½ hours, or until the meat is fork-tender. Serve immediately.

Some things never change. For example, back in the 1930s, there weren't too many things you could be sure of (except, like today, death and taxes!). But there was one sure thing we could count on at our house, and that was that Mom would always whip up her incredible mashed potatoes to go along with her Swiss steak. Mmm!!

Mom would fill a big aluminum pot with potatoes, water, and some salt, and it would boil and boil on our gas stove. I had an important job to do for Mom. Oh, I didn't have to peel the potatoes—I was her official taster! Mom usually boiled an extra pound or two since she knew how much I liked to sample those potatoes.

Now, even though this recipe has the old-fashioned flavor of Mom's, it's a little bit different. When Mom served these with her Swiss steak, she made them with a generous amount of chicken fat (homemade, of course) instead of the milk and butter. And she didn't bake them, either. But with today's food safety standards, I decided it's best to bake the finished dish since, otherwise, the egg might not be totally cooked. Mom sure would be proud!

Old-fashioned Mashed Potatoes

4 to 6 servings

4 pounds potatoes, peeled and cut
    into large chunks
1 egg, beaten
⅓ cup butter

½ cup milk
2 teaspoons salt
½ teaspoon black pepper

Place the potatoes in a large pot and add just enough water to cover them. Bring to a boil over high heat, then reduce the heat to medium and continue cooking for 20 to 25 minutes, or until fork-tender. Preheat the oven to 350°F. Drain the potatoes and place in a large bowl; add the remaining ingredients and beat with an electric beater on medium speed until smooth. Place in a 2-quart casserole dish that has been coated with nonstick vegetable spray, cover, and bake for 15 to 20 minutes, until warmed through.

Dad was the primary food shopper for our family. He'd bring home meat from the butcher shop, produce from local farmers, and fish. Yup, every week Dad would bring home some kind of local fish. Usually he'd get it at the Mohican Market. And when he asked me to go along with him, you betcha I went! I loved that place! I can still remember being nose-high to the counters. And the smell . . . ! You could say those are "strong" memories!

Mom would clean the fish and cook it up with lots of onions. You know, Mom believed in cooking just about everything with lots of onions. She said onions give food real flavor, and, to this day, I sure agree.

Oniony Skillet Fish Fillets

4 servings

½ cup vegetable oil
3 medium-sized onions, thinly sliced
1 pound fresh or frozen white-fleshed fish fillets, such as cod, haddock, or whiting, thawed if frozen, cut into 4-inch pieces

½ cup all-purpose flour
2 eggs, beaten

Preheat the oven to 200°F. In a large skillet, heat the oil over medium-high heat. Add the onions and sauté for 18 to 20 minutes, or until browned. Using a slotted spoon, remove the onions to an oven-proof platter, cover, and place in the oven to keep warm. Set the skillet aside. Place the flour in a shallow dish; place the beaten eggs in another shallow dish. Coat the fish evenly on both sides with the flour; coat with the egg, then coat again with the flour. Rewarm the oil remaining in the skillet over medium heat and sauté the fish, a few pieces at a time, for 4 to 6 minutes, until golden brown on both sides, turning halfway through the cooking. (The time may vary depending upon the thickness of the fillets.) Place the cooked fillets on a paper towel–lined baking sheet to drain; transfer the fish to a serving platter and top with the browned onions just before serving.

Growing up in Troy, I had the best of both worlds. I lived right near the hustle and bustle of downtown, yet I had friends who lived close by in the country. Sometimes I thought I was missing out by not waking up to the sound of roosters crowing and cows mooing. That was until it hit me that I woke up to a rooster and cow every morning, too—except my rooster was on the Kellogg's® cereal box and the cow part . . . well, you get it.

Not only did we eat Kellogg's Corn Flakes® for breakfast, but Mom would often mix them into her ground meat or sprinkle them on casseroles. Those are some of the good old basics that my grandchildren enjoy even today.

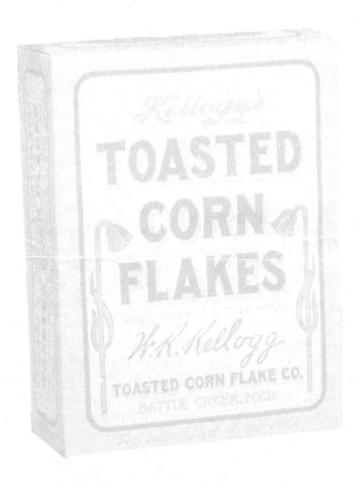

Creamy Spinach Bake

4 to 6 servings

5 tablespoons butter or margarine
3 cups Kellogg's Corn Flakes® cereal, crushed to 1½ cups, divided
3 tablespoons chopped onion
2 tablespoons all-purpose flour
¼ teaspoon salt

1¼ cups skim milk
1 cup (4 ounces) shredded Swiss cheese
1 package (10 ounces) frozen chopped spinach, thawed and squeezed dry
2 eggs, well beaten

Preheat the oven to 350°F. In a large saucepan, melt the butter over low heat. Remove 2 tablespoons to a large bowl and add ¾ cup cereal; mix well, and set aside for the topping. Stir the onion, flour, and salt into the butter remaining in the pan. Cook for about 1 minute, stirring constantly. Gradually add the milk, stirring until smooth. Increase the heat to medium and cook until the mixture comes to a boil, stirring constantly. Remove from the heat. Add the cheese, stirring until slightly melted. Stir in the spinach, eggs, and the remaining ¾ cup cereal. Spread the mixture in a 1-quart casserole dish. Sprinkle the reserved cereal topping over the spinach mixture. Bake for about 25 minutes, or until heated through.

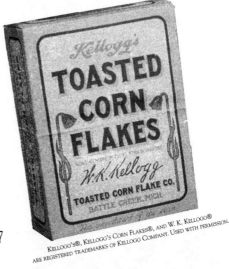

17

I was cutting meat and manning the shop. . . .

As I got older, I started helping Dad in his butcher shop. I was a good *schlepper,* which means I got to do the heavy lugging for him. I also got to pick the feathers off the chickens and turkeys. But by the time I was 14, I was cutting meat and manning the shop after school and on Sundays while Dad made deliveries in our pickup truck. When I worked with him on Sundays, boy did we have great lunches! We'd grill 2 or 3 steaks for each of us in a hinged grill basket over the coals in our potbelly stove. We'd have them with lots of ketchup. And sometimes we'd have an extra veal chop or two on hand, so we'd throw that in, too, covered with mustard and a load of black pepper. Today I make something similar on the barbecue grill. Unfortunately, something's missing: Dad's grin, as I gobble these up.

Butcher Shop Veal Chops

4 servings

½ cup deli-style mustard
1½ tablespoons whole black
    peppercorns, cracked

4 veal rib chops
    (8 to 10 ounces each)

Preheat the grill to medium-high heat. In a small bowl, combine the mustard and pepper. Coat the veal completely with the mixture, spreading it thick, and grill for 14 to 16 minutes, or to desired doneness, turning halfway through the grilling.

NOTE: The easiest way to crack peppercorns is to seal them in a resealable plastic storage bag and crack with a rolling pin. You could also use black pepper that you grind yourself right from the peppermill. Either way, your chops will have that really fresh cracked-pepper taste.

You know how we all grow up thinking we're so different from our parents? Well, I sure did. My dad had this habit of bringing home lots of food at one time. He never brought home just 4 or 6 tomatoes or potatoes. It was always a bushel of them or a burlap sack of carrots or sweet potatoes. Well, my family accuses me of being the same way now! I love to go to the farmers' market and get a whole sack of corn or beans. Then I have some to bring home and enjoy with Ethel, and more to share with my kids and their growing families. If they think I'm just like my father because of that, I admit I'm guilty!

Oh—thinking about all those sacks of carrots and sweet potatoes reminds me of how my sister, Flo, and I would look at each other when Dad brought *those* in the house. Know why? We knew it was tzimmes time! Actually, it was tzimmes-*making* time. Since Mom let it cook and cook and cook some more, it wasn't actually tzimmes-*eating* time for a while. But that was okay—'cause it was worth the wait.

SIDE DISHES

Tzimmes

6 to 8 servings

2 cans (29 ounces each) sweet
   potatoes, drained
2 cans (14½ ounces each) whole
   carrots, drained
1 package (12 ounces) pitted prunes

¾ cup honey
½ cup orange juice
¼ cup (½ stick) butter, melted
1 teaspoon salt

Preheat the oven to 350°F. In a 2-quart casserole dish that has been coated with nonstick vegetable spray, combine all the ingredients; mix well. Bake, uncovered, for 1½ hours, or until heated through, stirring occasionally.

Summer was the only time that the weather in Troy was practically perfect. And when summer came, I got to ride along with Dad when he took his butchered meat out into the country to trade with farmers for bushels of fresh fruit and vegetables. I loved bumping down those gravel roads with him. And I loved smelling and tasting that fresh produce. You couldn't get it any fresher!

The summer favorite around my house was corn on the cob. After Dad and I got the fresh corn home, it was my job to husk it. And, talk about anticipation! When Mom boiled up the first corn of the season, Flo and I would stand there waiting for it to cool off after Mom took it out of her huge corn pot. We'd butter it and salt it and end up eating those first ears right over the kitchen sink, with butter dripping down our chins!

We each ate at least 2 or 3 ears (or 5 or 6!) that way, and if there were any leftovers that we didn't eat cold the next day right off the cob, Mom would use the rest for her yummy corn soup or corn relish. The homegrown corn season sure brings back memories every year . . . as if all of this happened just yesterday. But now I get to enjoy watching the butter run down my grandchildrens' chins.

The homegrown corn season sure brings back memories every year. . . .

Corn Relish

6 to 8 servings

⅓ cup vegetable oil
¼ cup cider vinegar
¼ cup chopped fresh parsley
2 teaspoons sugar
½ teaspoon dried basil
¼ teaspoon cayenne pepper

2 large tomatoes, coarsely chopped
1 green bell pepper, chopped
3 scallions, chopped
2 cans (15 ounces each) whole kernel corn, drained (see Note)

In a large bowl, combine the oil, vinegar, parsley, sugar, basil, and cayenne pepper; mix well. Add the remaining ingredients and stir until well combined. Cover and chill for several hours, or overnight, before serving.

NOTE: My mom made this with the kernels she cut from 6 ears of left-over cooked corn. Even though she made it completely from scratch, sometimes I like to simplify things a bit by substituting ⅔ cup Italian dressing for the oil, vinegar, and basil.

Summer turned to fall, harvest season came, and the apple orchards treated us with the sweetest, crispest apples you could imagine. Boy, were we lucky to live within a few miles of some of the best orchards. We'd pick and bring home bushels and bushels of those beauties . . . so many that they filled our back porch! Fortunately, Mom was used to it from living with Dad all those years. And she knew what she had to do. She'd get right to work turning those McIntosh and Cortlands into all of our favorites, from applesauce to apple crisp, and, my absolute favorite, baked apples. The best part of those was the syrup that hardened on the bottom of the pan. It was kind of like a caramel apple. Usually I topped mine off with milk or cream. Boy, is that good! Now you know why autumn was such a popular season at my house.

You know, it didn't matter to Mom what type of apple she used for what. Back then, an apple was an apple, and if we wanted one for eating or baking, we used whatever we had. But today, different types of apples are suggested for different uses. You can check my apple guide on page 25 or do what Mom did, and use whatever you've got on hand.

Baked Apples

6 servings

6 Granny Smith, Cortland,
   Golden Delicious, or other
   baking apples
⅓ cup firmly packed light brown
   sugar

1 teaspoon ground cinnamon
3 tablespoons butter
¼ cup water

Preheat the oven to 325°F. Core the apples three quarters of the way through, leaving the bottoms intact. Score each apple horizontally around the middle to allow for expansion during baking (see illustration below). In a small bowl, combine the brown sugar and cinnamon. Reserve 1 teaspoon of the mixture and spoon the remaining mixture evenly into the cored centers of the apples; press 1½ teaspoons of butter over each. Place the apples open end up in an 8-inch square baking dish. Sprinkle the reserved teaspoon of the sugar mixture evenly over the tops of the apples. Put the water in the bottom of the baking dish, then cover tightly with aluminum foil. Bake for 40 to 45 minutes, or until the apples can be pierced easily with a fork.

APPLE GUIDE

Here's a quick guide that tells you the best apples for snacking, baking, and making candy or caramel apples. Of course you can use your favorites, but this helps when you want to make the most of your fresh apples. For example, the apples suggested for applesauce are those that stay the most flavorful when cooked. For baked apples, you should choose ones that hold their shape and get richer-tasting when baked. For breads, cakes, and muffins, you do best with apples that keep their shape and have both tart and sweet flavor; for pies, cobblers, and crisps, the best are the ones that retain their texture and flavor through long baking; and for candy and caramel apples, the best are those that stay crunchy under sweet coatings. For eating raw, well . . . the ones I suggest are sweet, crisp, and juicy—but go with what you and your family like the best.

Apple	Best Use(s)
Cortland	Eating raw, and for baked apples, pies, cobblers, and crisps
Crispin	Breads, cakes, muffins, and pastries
Empire	Eating raw
Fuji	Eating raw
Gala	Eating raw
Golden Delicious	Baked apples, pies, cobblers, crisps, breads, cakes, muffins, and pastries
Granny Smith	Eating raw, and for breads, cakes, muffins, pastries, baked apples, pies, cobblers, and crisps
Jonathan	Applesauce
Macoun	Applesauce and candy and caramel apples
McIntosh	Eating raw, and for applesauce and candy and caramel apples
Newtown Pippin	Applesauce, pies, cobblers, and crisps
Red Delicious	Eating raw
Rome Beauty	Applesauce, baked apples, breads, cakes, muffins, and pastries
Winesap	Eating raw, and for applesauce, breads, cakes, muffins, and pastries

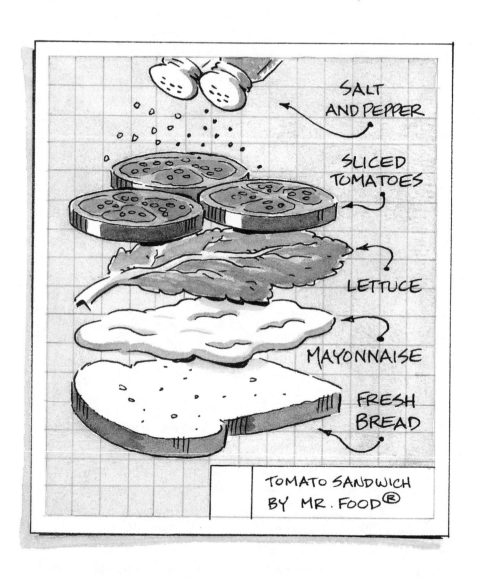

SALT AND PEPPER

SLICED TOMATOES

LETTUCE

MAYONNAISE

FRESH BREAD

TOMATO SANDWICH BY MR. FOOD®

When somebody asks you what your favorite food is, do you have to think about it? Maybe it's a rich pot roast or a gooey dessert? Well, whenever somebody asks me what *my* favorite food is (and that happens a lot!), I answer in a flash . . . "A tomato sandwich!"

Hard to believe?! Well, I have to confess—I like almost all foods. So, the name Mr. Food sure fits. But my all-time favorite food is a basic tomato sandwich. Mmm, hmm. Boy, do I love fresh-from-the-garden tomatoes sliced and piled on a hearty rye or country-style bread, topped with a piece of crispy lettuce, dolloped with some mayonnaise, and sprinkled with a little salt and pepper. (If you don't believe it's this simple, check out the diagram . . . and taste the heavenly results!)

Oh, did I mention that no tomato sandwich is complete without washing it down with a big glass of milk? Tomato sandwiches were a popular lunch choice—and even a snack, too, while I was growing up. So, in those days, I'd finish one off with at least a quart of ice-cold milk. And every time I snuck a quick sandwich between meals, Mom could tell. My milk mustache gave me away!

SANDWICHES

My Favorite Tomato Sandwich

6 sandwiches

⅓ cup mayonnaise
12 slices country-style white bread
6 romaine lettuce leaves, washed
    and dried

3 large homegrown-style tomatoes,
    cut into ½-inch-thick slices
Salt and black pepper to taste

Spread the mayonnaise evenly on one side of each slice of bread. Place the lettuce leaves over the mayonnaise on 6 of the slices, then place the tomato slices over the lettuce. Sprinkle with salt and pepper to taste, then top with the remaining bread. Slice in half and enjoy!

Okay, so a tomato sandwich is my favorite food. But the runner-up is . . . (drum roll, please) a cheese sandwich! Yup, I've always been a cheese lover. And when I bite into a sandwich made with thick slices cut right off a block of smooth, white, old-fashioned American cheese, I'm in sandwich heaven. It takes me back to the days when Dad would bring home bricks of cheese in wooden boxes.

Actually, I've gotten adventurous in recent years. I've mixed and matched all different cheeses, both hard and soft, with a variety of breads and rolls and with spreads ranging from plain and flavored mayonnaise to loads of different types of mustards. The cheese and condiment selections we have today are amazing—and I try to take advantage of all of them!

SANDWICHES

My Favorite Cheese Sandwich

4 sandwiches

¼ cup prepared yellow mustard
4 kaiser rolls, split
4 iceberg lettuce leaves, washed and dried

12 slices (1 ounce each) American cheese

Spread the mustard evenly over the cut sides of the kaiser rolls. Place a lettuce leaf on the bottom half of each roll and top each with 3 slices of cheese. Place the roll tops over the cheese and serve.

NOTE: Although nothing could be simpler than a cheese sandwich, it's still one of my favorites. Experiment and see which kind of cheese sandwich is your favorite—after all, the possibilities are virtually endless, depending on the type of bread, the cheese, the mustard, and the other condiments you choose. I love them all!

My sister, Flo, is 10 years older than me. And to this day, she still reminds me that wherever she went during her teen years, she always had me tagging along. Poor Flo! She was like my second mom, and now that we're older, we can look back and realize how much she really helped Mom.

Not only did Flo take care of me, but she did her share of the kitchen work, too. Today she's glad, 'cause she's an excellent cook. But in those days, she handled loads of responsibilities around the house. From as far back as I can remember, it was Flo's job to handle the dinner vegetables. We didn't have prepared bagged salads in the '30s and '40s, either! No way! Our choice of salad greens was pretty much limited to iceberg lettuce. Flo cut the tomatoes and cucumbers to go along with it, then she topped it all—or should I say, smothered it—with homemade Russian dressing. I still like that dressing so much that it's my all-purpose dressing. If you're like me, you'll put it on almost anything!

DRESSINGS

Flo's Russian Dressing

about 2½ cups

2 cups mayonnaise
¼ cup ketchup
½ cup sweet pickle relish

½ teaspoon garlic powder
½ teaspoon salt
½ teaspoon black pepper

In a medium-sized bowl, combine all the ingredients until thoroughly mixed. Serve immediately, or cover and chill until ready to use.

Canned food was sweeping the country in the 1940s. It was convenient (still is!) and shelf-stable (still is!). People used these "revolutionary" new products to help out in the kitchen. Canned soups were big hits because not only could they be used as quick soups, but they also went into making easy sauces and gravies. And when Campbell's came out with this recipe for a cake that used their tomato soup, people went nuts over it!

I've received lots of requests for this recipe over the years, since people remember their moms and grandmas making it. I went straight to Campbell's to get the original version and, know what? It's as moist and yummy today as I remember it. See who you can surprise with the secret ingredient!

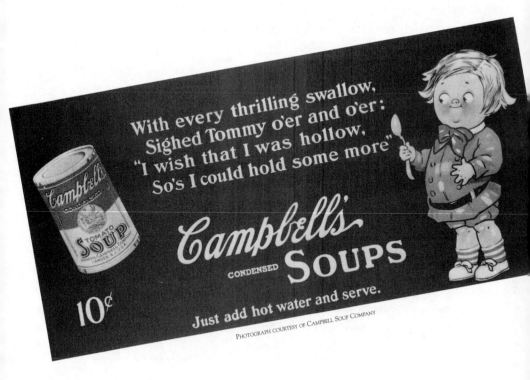

PHOTOGRAPH COURTESY OF CAMPBELL SOUP COMPANY

Tomato Soup–Spice Cake

12 to 15 servings

2 cups all-purpose flour
1⅓ cups sugar
4 teaspoons baking powder
1 teaspoon baking soda
1½ teaspoons ground allspice
1 teaspoon ground cinnamon

½ teaspoon ground cloves
1 can (10¾ ounces) Campbell's
    Condensed Tomato Soup
½ cup vegetable shortening
2 eggs
¼ cup water

Preheat the oven to 350°F. In a large bowl, combine the flour, sugar, baking powder, baking soda, allspice, cinnamon, and cloves. Add the remaining ingredients and beat with an electric beater on low speed until well mixed, scraping down the sides of the bowl as necessary. Increase the speed to high and beat for 4 more minutes. Pour the batter into a 9" × 13" baking pan that has been coated with nonstick baking spray and lightly floured. Bake for 35 to 40 minutes, or until a wooden toothpick inserted in the center comes out clean. Cool in the pan on a wire rack.

NOTE: Frost with Cream Cheese Frosting, if desired.

Cream Cheese Frosting

about 3 cups

1 package (8 ounces) cream
    cheese, softened
2 tablespoons milk

1 teaspoon vanilla extract
2½ cups confectioners' sugar

In a medium-sized bowl, with an electric beater on medium speed, beat the cream cheese, milk, and vanilla until creamy. Gradually beat in the confectioners' sugar until smooth. Use to frost completely cooled cakes, cupcakes, or other goodies.

Do you think it's true that food likes are hereditary? As a kid, I remember picking berries at Mr. Hayner's farm—blueberries, strawberries, blackberries—buckets of them! We'd get home and clean them up and eat them in a bowl, topped with a little milk and sugar. Mmm! Or Mom would make berry cobbler or berry anything. Her favorite was blueberry crumb pie, and, boy, you can be sure that Flo and I finished our dinners quickly on those nights so that we could dig into nice big pieces of pie!

I know that my mom's special love for blueberries was passed down to my three kids, especially my son Steve. I remember taking him with me to tape a show in the blueberry fields of Hammonton, New Jersey, in my early days as Mr. Food. Somehow, Steve managed to wander off in the fields and, when I finally found him, his purple lips and hands told me the whole story. I guess you could say he had guilt written all over his face, and it took a few days for his blueberry smile to disappear! Next time, I think I'll take my son Chuck.

THE TIMES RECORD, TROY, N. Y., WEDNESDAY EVENING, MARCH 19, 1941.

Cast Which Presented "Ideal Gym Day"

No-Roll Crumb Pie Crust

One 10-inch deep-dish pie crust

3 cups all-purpose flour
1 cup sugar
1 teaspoon salt

1 cup (2 sticks) butter, cut into
  chunks

In a large bowl, combine the flour, sugar, and salt. Cut in the butter with a pastry cutter or 2 knives until crumbly. Place half of the mixture in a 10-inch deep-dish pie plate that has been coated with nonstick baking spray. Press the mixture firmly with your fingers over the bottom and up the sides to form a crust. Fill the crust with your desired pie filling. Sprinkle the remaining crumbs over the pie filling and bake according to the filling instructions, or until the crumbs are golden and the filling is bubbly.

Blueberry Crumb Pie

8 servings

2 cans (21 ounces each) blueberry
  pie filling
1 pint fresh blueberries, washed

1 No-Roll Crumb Pie Crust

Preheat the oven to 425°F. In a large bowl, combine the pie filling and blueberries; gently stir or toss until well combined. Pour into the prepared crust and top with the remaining crumbs. Bake for 45 to 50 minutes, or until the crumbs are golden and the filling is bubbly.

Bake, bake, bake. Mom and her oven were always going strong. She didn't bake cupcakes or chocolate chip cookies. No, her recipes were really traditional ones. Her mandel bread was always a winner. I think mandel bread was a "mom" thing in the '40s, since all my friends' moms made it, no matter what their heritage. My Italian friends called it *biscotti,* and that's what most of us know it as today.

In those days we ate it one of two ways—either cut cake-style or sliced and toasted in the oven until it got really crunchy (the way today's biscotti are made). That way they got so hard that Flo and I joked that we could use them as doorstops! Sure, we laughed about them, but we sure gobbled them up.

I'll never forget Mom dunking her mandel bread into her tea after dinner. Now, it was just regular plain tea that she made in those days—there weren't any flavor choices like we have today. But you know what she did? She'd always find something to dissolve in her tea to give it a little flavor—a spoonful of jam or honey, or even a bit of flavored gelatin. Oh, how she loved to linger over her nightly tea before cleaning up the dinner dishes. Biscotti has become really popular today, and every time I see it, I think of Mom dunking slices of mandel bread into her own flavored tea.

Dunkin' Mandel Bread

about 18 slices

3 eggs
¾ cup plus 1 tablespoon sugar, divided
1 cup vegetable oil
3 cups all-purpose flour

2½ teaspoons baking powder
1 cup chopped walnuts
1 teaspoon vanilla extract
½ teaspoon lemon extract
¼ teaspoon ground cinnamon

Preheat the oven to 325°F. Place the eggs in a large bowl and beat lightly; add ¾ cup sugar and mix well with a spoon. Stir in the oil, then add the flour and baking powder; mix until thoroughly combined. Add the nuts; mix well. Mix in the vanilla and lemon extracts; the mixture will be sticky. Divide the dough in half and place each piece on a baking sheet that has been coated with nonstick baking spray. Form each into an oval about 4" × 9". In a small bowl, combine the remaining 1 tablespoon sugar with the cinnamon and sprinkle over the tops of the dough. Bake for 20 to 25 minutes, or until golden brown. Allow to cool and slice 1 inch thick.

NOTE: For a crisper mandel bread, place the slices on rimmed baking sheets and bake for an additional 15 minutes per side.

I was lucky to grow up surrounded by the love of my mom, dad, sister, and lots of aunts, uncles, and cousins. Unfortunately, my grandparents didn't live long enough for me to remember them. But I do remember hearing lots of stories about them— especially Bubbie Rachel, my mom's mother.

I heard about Bubbie Rachel so much that I felt as if I'd known her. And Mom sure kept her memory alive by making Bubbie's special babka for us, often. Oh, the smell of that rich babka baking! Mom passed the recipe down to us and Ethel still makes it for the family once in a while. When she does, that incredible aroma brings back such wonderful memories of Mom and her stories about Bubbie. If only Bubbie could know how much a part of her family she still is. . . .

1945

Lloyd
Troy N.Y.

37

Bubbie's Babka

10 servings

¼ cup plus 1 tablespoon water, divided
½ cup granulated sugar, divided
¾ cup milk
1½ teaspoons salt
1 package (¼ ounce) active dry yeast
1 egg
3¼ cups all-purpose flour, divided

¼ cup vegetable oil
1¼ teaspoons vanilla extract, divided
Nonstick baking spray
2 tablespoons butter, melted
1 tablespoon ground cinnamon
¼ cup chopped walnuts
¾ cup confectioners' sugar

In a medium-sized saucepan, heat ¼ cup water, ¼ cup granulated sugar, the milk, and salt over medium heat until the mixture is steaming but not boiling. Remove from the heat and allow to cool until lukewarm. Add the yeast and let sit for 3 to 4 minutes, until foamy. Add the egg; mix well. Place 3 cups flour in a large bowl, then add the milk mixture and stir just until moistened. Add the oil and 1 teaspoon vanilla; mix until a soft dough is formed. Dust a clean countertop with 2 tablespoons flour. Knead the dough on the floured surface for 3 to 5 minutes, or until smooth and elastic. Shape the dough into a ball and place in a large bowl that has been coated with nonstick baking spray. Spray the top of the dough with nonstick baking spray, cover with plastic wrap, and place in a warm place for 2 hours, or until doubled in size.

Flour a clean work surface with the remaining 2 tablespoons flour. Punch down the dough and place on the floured surface, then shape the dough into a rectangle about 8" × 12". Brush with the melted butter. In a small bowl, combine the remaining ¼ cup granulated sugar and the cinnamon. Sprinkle over the top of the dough, then sprinkle with the walnuts. Starting from a long side, roll up the dough jelly-roll fashion and place seam side down in a 12-cup Bundt pan that has been coated with non-stick baking spray. Overlap the ends and pinch them together, forming a solid ring. Spray the dough with nonstick baking spray. Cover with plastic wrap and let rise in a warm place until doubled in size, about 2 hours. Preheat the oven to 400°F. Uncover the pan and bake for 20 to 25 minutes, or until golden brown. Remove from the pan and cool on a wire rack for 5 minutes. In a small bowl, combine the remaining 1 tablespoon water, ¼ teaspoon vanilla, and the confectioners' sugar. Drizzle over the top of the babka while still warm. Serve warm, or allow to cool, then serve.

High School Diploma

This Certifies That

Arthur J. Ginsburg

having honorably completed the

Academic

Course of Study is hereby declared a graduate of the

Troy High School

In Witness Whereof, *we have hereunto subscribed our names at Troy, New York, this* 29th *day of* June 1949.

Charles H. Connolly
Superintendent

Dudley P. Van _____
Secretary

_____
President of Board

W. Kenneth Doyle
Principal

AFTER-SCHOOL ACTIVITIES

Boy, my high school years sure hold a special place in my memories—the sporting events, the proms (oh, the stories I wish I could share), and, of course, the food! Well, you know how important food is to kids in high school . . . at least it was to us. Food was the center of our social lives. After school, sports practice, or a game, it was normal for us to grab a snack and hang out together downtown before going home.

When we wanted a quick snack, we'd get ice cream sodas at Sliter's Dairy or Tornecello's. I loved sipping from paper straws that stuck out of those tall glasses in the metal holders. We used to have races to see who could get to the bottom of the glass first. Ooh, the ice cream headaches we'd have! You should have seen the heads turn as a bunch of us sat at the counter, slurping down our sodas. We were louder than the Andrews Sisters singing "Accentuate the Positive" on the jukebox!

Brown Cow Milk Shake

5 to 6 servings

3 cups chocolate ice cream   ½ cup chocolate-flavored syrup
1½ cups milk

Combine all the ingredients in a blender and blend for 1 to 1½ minutes, or until smooth and thick. Serve in tall glasses (with straws, of course).

NOTE: If you prefer a thinner shake, use an additional ½ cup milk.

Memory Lane Milk Shake

5 servings

2½ cups vanilla ice cream   1¼ cups milk
2 cups frozen strawberries (about   ½ cup sugar
⅔ of a 16-ounce package)   5 fresh strawberries, washed

Combine all the ingredients except the fresh strawberries in a blender. Blend on high speed until smooth. Pour into tall glasses and top each with a fresh strawberry.

NOTE: These are so thick that you'll need to serve them with straws *and* spoons!

We've all heard the tall tales of fishermen bragging about "the one that got away" and the "record-breaking catch." Well, I've done my share of fishing, too. In fact, here I am on a fishing trip to Saratoga Lake with my best buddy, Stan Falk. What a pair!

Unfortunately, most of my fishing stories don't have successful endings—except that I always had lots of fun! But when it came to *eating* fish, well, that's a different story. All it took was a quick trip to Gallagher's Fish Fry in Watervliet to make us wonder why we ever went fishing ourselves! There was nothing like their strips of moist, flaky white fish served up in hot dog buns. Sometimes we had them topped with a spicy chili sauce, other times we had tartar sauce. I've never quite been able to exactly duplicate their fried fish and sauces, but these recipes come pretty close. Try them once and I bet you'll be hooked, too!

My best buddy, Stan Falk, and me at Saratoga Lake.

Fish-Fry Sandwiches

4 sandwiches

¼ cup all-purpose flour
2 eggs, beaten
1 cup seasoned dry bread crumbs
½ cup vegetable or peanut oil

1 pound fresh or frozen white-fleshed fish fillets, such as cod, haddock, or whiting, thawed if frozen, cut in half lengthwise
4 hot dog buns, split

Place the flour, beaten eggs, and bread crumbs in three separate shallow dishes. Heat the oil in a large skillet over medium heat until hot but not smoking. Coat the fish evenly with the flour, then the egg, then the bread crumbs. Fry in the hot oil for 4 to 6 minutes, until golden brown on both sides and the fish flakes easily with a fork, turning about halfway through the frying. (The cooking time may vary depending upon the thickness of the fillets.) Drain on paper towels and serve on the buns.

NOTE: Gallagher's Fish Fry used to serve these with a red chili sauce that gave them a real zing. Today when we make them at home, my family enjoys them with the Tartar Sauce below.

Zippy Tartar Sauce

about 1½ cups

1 cup mayonnaise
¾ cup sweet pickle relish, drained
¼ cup finely chopped sweet onion
   (see Note)

Juice of ½ lemon

In a small bowl, combine the mayonnaise, relish, and onion; mix well. Add the lemon juice and stir until well combined. Serve immediately, or cover and chill until ready to use.

NOTE: Today we're really lucky to have a variety of sweet onions available, and any of them will work here—from Vidalias to Texas 1015s, Mauis, and Walla Wallas. Or just use red onions if these aren't available.

"Watch out, Troy High football rivals! Big Art Ginsburg's on *our* team!" Yeah, I was a hard-hitting player in those days. I was in great shape at 225 pounds, and, naturally, it was important to keep my weight up during the season. That wasn't a problem, since my appetite was never-ending.

After games, a bunch of us guys would go out for Italian food. I'd order lasagna, which would take about 20 minutes to prepare. Well, I was ravenous, so, while I waited for the lasagna, I'd have a hot meatball sandwich smothered in a rich red sauce, then a big cheese pizza. See why keeping my weight up wasn't a problem?! Our team had a pretty good record, so I'd like to think that eating all that Italian food had winning results!

Hot Meatball Sandwiches

4 sandwiches

½ pound hot Italian sausage,
  casings removed
½ pound ground beef
2 eggs
¾ cup Italian-style or seasoned
  dry bread crumbs
2 tablespoons grated Parmesan cheese
1 teaspoon salt

¼ teaspoon black pepper
1 tablespoon vegetable oil
1 jar (26 ounces) spaghetti sauce
½ cup water
4 hoagie or hero rolls, split

In a large bowl, combine the sausage, ground beef, eggs, bread crumbs, cheese, salt, and pepper; mix well. Form into twelve 1½-inch meatballs. Heat the oil in a large saucepan over medium heat and cook the meatballs for 6 to 8 minutes, gently turning occasionally to brown on all sides. Add the spaghetti sauce and water; reduce the heat to low, cover, and cook for 45 to 50 minutes, or until the meatballs are no longer pink, stirring occasionally. Place 3 meatballs on each hoagie roll. Spoon sauce evenly over the meatballs and place the remaining sauce in a bowl to serve along with the sandwiches; serve immediately.

Memorable Sicilian Pizza

12 servings

1 pound store-bought pizza dough
1 can (8 ounces) tomato sauce
1 teaspoon dried oregano
1 teaspoon dried basil
½ teaspoon garlic powder
¼ teaspoon onion powder
¼ teaspoon sugar
⅛ teaspoon black pepper
2 cups (8 ounces) shredded
   mozzarella cheese
¼ cup grated Parmesan cheese

Preheat the oven to 450°F. Using your fingertips or the heel of your hand, spread the dough to cover the bottom of a 10" × 15" rimmed baking sheet that has been coated with nonstick vegetable spray. In a small bowl, combine the tomato sauce, oregano, basil, garlic powder, onion powder, sugar, and pepper; mix well. Spoon evenly over the dough and sprinkle with the mozzarella cheese, then the Parmesan cheese. Bake for 15 to 17 minutes, or until the crust is lightly browned and the cheese is bubbly.

Worth-the-Wait Lasagna

9 to 12 servings

1 package (16 ounces) lasagna
   noodles
1 pound hot Italian sausage,
   casings removed
1 container (15 ounces) ricotta
   cheese
1 egg

⅓ cup grated Parmesan cheese
½ teaspoon dried basil
¼ teaspoon black pepper
4 cups (16 ounces) shredded
   mozzarella cheese, divided
2 jars (26 ounces each) spaghetti
   sauce

Preheat the oven to 375°F. Cook the lasagna noodles according to the package directions; drain, rinse, and drain again. In a large skillet, brown the sausage over medium-high heat, until crumbled and no pink remains. Drain off the excess liquid and set aside to cool slightly. In a large bowl, combine the ricotta cheese, egg, Parmesan cheese, basil, pepper, cooled sausage, and 3 cups mozzarella cheese; mix well. Coat a 9" × 13" glass baking dish with nonstick vegetable spray. Spread 1 cup spaghetti sauce evenly over the bottom of the dish. Place 3 noodles over the sauce. Sprinkle one third of the cheese mixture evenly over the noodles. Pour 1 cup spaghetti sauce over the cheese mixture. Place 3 more noodles over the top and press down lightly. Repeat with 2 more layers of the cheese mixture, sauce, and noodles. Spoon the remaining sauce over the top and cover tightly with aluminum foil. Bake for 1 hour. Remove the foil and sprinkle the remaining 1 cup mozzarella cheese over the top; return to the oven for 5 minutes, or until the cheese has melted. Remove from the oven and allow to sit for 10 to 15 minutes; cut and serve.

In the late 1940s and early 1950s, foreign food, as it was called then, became popular here. Chinese restaurants were popping up all over the country, and I remember my first taste of Chinese food. I was 16 years old when a few friends and I found this little restaurant with Chinese writing on the front door on South Pearl Street in downtown Albany. We had wonton soup, egg rolls, and chicken chow mein. I couldn't get enough! No, I didn't use chopsticks then—I used a fork, although the way I was eating, I could have used a shovel! The only thing that slowed me down was the hot mustard. Wow, did that get me!

If the fortune-cookie–saying writer had known me personally, my fortune probably would have said something like, "To eat is to enjoy," because I did then and I *still* do!

Chicken Chow Mein

4 servings

4 teaspoons soy sauce
1 can (14½ ounces) ready-to-use
    chicken broth, divided
2 celery stalks, sliced ¼ inch thick
2 large carrots, sliced ¼ inch thick
1 small onion, cut in half and sliced

1 can (8 ounces) water chestnuts,
    drained
1 can (16 ounces) bean sprouts,
    drained
2 tablespoons cornstarch
2 cups cubed cooked chicken

In a medium-sized saucepan, combine the soy sauce and all but 3 tablespoons of the chicken broth over medium-high heat. Add the celery, carrots, and onion and cook for about 10 minutes, until tender. Stir in the water chestnuts and bean sprouts. In a small bowl, combine the cornstarch and the reserved 3 tablespoons chicken broth; add to the vegetable mixture and stir until the liquid thickens. Add the chicken and mix well; cook for 3 to 4 minutes, or until the chicken is heated through.

NOTE: Serve over cooked spaghetti or plain or fried rice, and top with crispy chow mein noodles.

If Dad didn't have to work, then summer Sunday afternoons meant one thing—picnic! Dad and I would clean out the back of the pickup truck while Mom and Flo packed a picnic lunch. They'd make sandwiches out of leftovers, so that usually meant meat loaf, chicken salad, or sliced brisket. And, of course, I could never forget our go-alongs. Mom would make potato salad with a generous amount of mayonnaise, and she'd pack it right back in the mayonnaise jar to take with us. Flo's specialty was coleslaw. That meant that she'd start from scratch by grating the cabbage by hand. She always made sure to show me her scraped knuckles, too! Did she make me feel guilty? Well, maybe a little bit, but I sure wouldn't let her know it!

It's a good thing mom's pickles were done in a jiffy, 'cause we wouldn't have been able to wait for them! She'd slice fresh Kirby cucumbers really thin, then toss them with just the right amount of vinegar and salt.

I would clean out the back of the pickup truck. . . .

51

These were Dad's favorites, so Mom made sure there were plenty. Then, off we'd go into the country to park along the side of a road and relax together. Oh, what simple times those were. . . .

Sunday Afternoon Pickles

about 7 cups

1 cup white vinegar
1 cup water
¾ cup sugar
1 teaspoon salt

8 cups peeled and thinly sliced Kirby or other cucumbers (about 3 pounds)

In a large bowl, combine the vinegar, water, sugar, and salt; mix well. Add the cucumbers and toss until well coated. Cover and chill for at least 2 hours, or overnight. These will keep in a sealed container in the refrigerator for several weeks.

NOTE: Sometimes Mom liked to spice it up a bit by adding a handful of chopped scallions or dillweed along with the cucumbers.

Picnic Potato Salad

8 to 10 servings

5 pounds potatoes, peeled and cut
  into 2-inch chunks
4 hard-boiled eggs, chopped
2 large celery stalks, chopped
  (about 1 cup)

1½ cups mayonnaise
1 teaspoon salt
½ teaspoon black pepper

Place the potatoes in a large pot and add just enough water to cover them. Bring to a boil over high heat, then reduce the heat to medium and cook for 20 to 25 minutes, or until the potatoes are fork-tender. Drain and allow to cool slightly. Transfer to a large bowl and add the remaining ingredients; toss well to coat. Serve immediately, or cover and chill until ready to serve.

Everything Coleslaw

about 4 cups

1 cup mayonnaise
Juice of 1 large lemon
3 tablespoons sugar
½ teaspoon celery seed
1 teaspoon salt

¼ teaspoon white pepper
6 cups shredded cabbage (1 small
  head—see Note)
1 cup shredded carrots (about
  2 carrots)

In a large bowl, combine the mayonnaise, lemon juice, sugar, celery seed, salt, and pepper. Add the shredded cabbage and carrots; toss to coat well. Cover and chill for 2 to 3 hours before serving.

NOTE: I like to use a combination of green and red cabbage (maybe 1 or 2 cups red and the rest green) to give this really bright color. You can also use two 10-ounce packages of preshredded coleslaw mix instead of shredding the cabbage and carrots yourself. It's a nice timesaver when you have little preparation time. (Too bad Flo didn't have that option!) Some say coleslaw should be sweet, others say it should be tangy. Well, it's easy to adjust the amount of sugar to your liking.

"Keep your elbows off the table," Dad would say, and, boy, did we listen! And, some nights, when Mom would bring out the tuna noodle casserole, Flo and I would laugh because *those* elbows—the elbow macaroni in the casserole—*were* allowed on the table.

Even Mom, who was used to cooking and baking every day, needed a break sometimes. And making this tuna noodle casserole was like a day off to her. Canned food was becoming really popular, so Mom would start us off with some canned tomato soup, then she'd serve the casserole, made with canned mushroom soup and canned tuna. I can still remember Dad bringing home some new kind of canned tuna from the wholesale market—not just one can, but a case of it, of course. It was from Japan and he had paid about 6¢ a can for it. We were amazed, because that was about 6¢ a can less than he had been paying up until then—and this new tuna was delicious, too! We had it in sandwiches and, of course, in our favorite casserole.

So, another thing that hasn't changed is that we can all appreciate a little help in the kitchen from convenience foods. (And tuna noodle casserole is *still* one of our family favorites!)

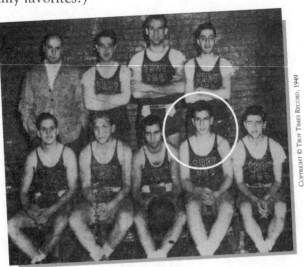

Family-Favorite Tuna Noodle Casserole

6 to 8 servings

1 package (16 ounces) elbow macaroni

1 can (12 ounces) water-packed tuna, drained and flaked

2 cans (10¾ ounces each) condensed cream of mushroom soup

1 can (8½ ounces) peas, drained

2 cups (8 ounces) shredded Swiss cheese, divided

1 cup heavy cream

¼ teaspoon black pepper

Preheat the oven to 350°F. Prepare the macaroni according to the package directions; drain, rinse, and drain again. Place in a large bowl and add the tuna, mushroom soup, peas, 1½ cups Swiss cheese, the cream, and pepper; mix well. Pour into a 9" × 13" baking dish that has been coated with nonstick vegetable spray. Sprinkle the remaining ½ cup cheese over the top. Bake for 20 to 25 minutes, or until heated through.

NOTE: When my mom made this recipe, she skimmed the heavy cream from the top of our fresh whole milk that Dad brought home right from the farm!

Besides going to school, playing sports, and getting into trouble, I made time to help around Dad's butcher shop. My bones still shiver when I think back to the cold November mornings when we'd drive an hour into the country to buy and slaughter turkeys for the holidays. In those days, people bought only the whole bird. They didn't have the option of buying parts, as we do today. So, here's what we did to get our beautiful holiday birds.

We had little or no heat in the pickup truck, and it's no secret that Troy, New York, has never been known for its warm winters! When we got to the farm, we'd put the turkeys in coops. It was my job to hold each turkey's wings just right during the slaughtering. Now, have you ever tried holding a 30-pound turkey by the wings? And tried to keep it still, no less?! Well, let me tell you, it's a real challenge. Dad would be there yelling at me to be careful. "Don't break the wings," he'd holler. "The bones are really sharp!" Just what I needed . . . more pressure. Actually, I knew going in there that broken turkey wing bones would have been sharp enough to slit my throat, so I really didn't need much reminding!

Well, I lived through it. And I guess those cold mornings were worth all that work, 'cause, boy, did we sell lots of turkeys for Thanksgiving, Christmas, and New Year's. And if there were any extras, Mom would smother ours with fresh garlic—inside and out—and roast it just like in this recipe. She'd serve it with all the trimmings, including homemade cranberry relish (not made in a food processor, though!).

Garlic-Roasted Turkey

6 to 8 servings

⅓ cup minced fresh garlic
¼ cup vegetable oil
1 teaspoon salt
½ teaspoon onion powder

½ teaspoon paprika
½ teaspoon black pepper
One 12- to 14-pound turkey

Preheat the oven to 325°F. In a medium-sized bowl, combine all the ingredients except the turkey; mix well. Loosen the skin from the turkey breast by slipping your hand between the breast and the skin; rub one third of the garlic mixture underneath the skin. Rub the remaining garlic mixture over the outside of the turkey. Place the turkey, breast side down, in a roasting pan filled with ¼ inch water. Bake for 1½ hours, then remove from the oven and carefully turn the turkey over so it is breast side up. Return to the oven and bake for an additional 2 to 2½ hours, or until no pink remains and the juices run clear.

Timetable for Roasting a Whole Turkey (at 325°F.)	
Approximate Weight (in pounds)	Approximate Roasting Time * (in hours)
6 to 8	2¼ to 3¼
8 to 12	3 to 4
12 to 16	3½ to 4½
16 to 20	4 to 5
20 to 24	4½ to 5½

*Approximate roasting time: Factors affecting roasting times are type of oven, oven temperature, and degree of thawing. Begin checking turkey for doneness about 1 hour before end of recommended roasting time.

Courtesy of the National Turkey Federation

Cranberry Relish

about 3 cups

1 package (12 ounces) fresh or
  frozen cranberries
1 medium-sized apple, unpeeled,
  cored and quartered

1 small seedless orange, unpeeled,
  quartered
1 cup sugar

In a food processor that has been fitted with its steel cutting blade, combine the cranberries, apple, and orange. Process until finely chopped, scraping down the sides of the bowl as necessary. Add the sugar and process until thoroughly combined. Place in a medium-sized glass serving bowl, cover, and chill for at least 1 hour before serving.

While I was in college, I lived at home. I mean, who could afford to move out?! Besides, I couldn't stand the thought of missing Mom's home cooking.

One day when I came home from class, Dad and our downstairs neighbor were talking . . . or maybe I could say, having a very loud discussion. Apparently, a homeless man had knocked on our neighbor's door and asked if he'd like to buy some potatoes and onions. Street peddling of produce wasn't uncommon in those days, so our neighbor paid the man for the potatoes and onions. The only problem was, he'd sold him *our* potatoes and onions! You see, we always kept our bushel baskets of potatoes and onions by our back door, which was next to our neighbor's back door.

Well, after he and our neighbor worked it out, Dad came upstairs and said he really couldn't stay angry, since the homeless man must have really needed the money. He brought home more potatoes and onions the next day so we wouldn't miss out on Mom's famous potato soup. These days, I make mine a little thicker than Mom's by adding instant potato flakes. It still has the rich taste of Mom's . . . and it really is easy!

Easy Potato Soup

6 to 8 servings

¼ cup (½ stick) butter
1 large onion, chopped
2 pounds potatoes, peeled and
  diced (about 4 cups)
1 medium-sized carrot, grated
2 cups water

1 teaspoon dried dillweed
1½ teaspoons salt
½ teaspoon black pepper
3 cups milk
1 cup instant potato flakes

In a soup pot, melt the butter over medium-high heat and sauté the onions for 6 to 8 minutes, until golden. Reduce the heat to low, add the potatoes, carrots, water, dillweed, salt, and pepper, and cook for 25 to 35 minutes, until the potatoes are fork-tender, stirring occasionally. Stir in the milk and bring to a boil over medium heat. Reduce the heat to low, add the potato flakes, and cook, stirring, until thickened. Serve immediately, or, if you desire a very creamy consistency, allow to simmer for 25 to 30 more minutes.

Most everybody did their own baking when I was growing up. There was little choice! We didn't have the access to ready-made baked goods that we have today. I remember Mom making 5 or 6 apple pies at a time. Sometimes I'd get hooked into helping peel the apples. Of course, I ate more than I peeled! Anyway, it was only fair that I helped, since I often invited a bunch of guys from the basketball team over for pie after practice.

In those days, the radiators had 2 settings—on and off. Sometimes they'd give off so much heat that we'd have to crack the windows to let some cool air in. Mom also cracked the windows when she set pies on the sills to cool. Since we lived on the second floor, that wasn't a problem—except that it was hard for me to wait for them to cool!

It was a different story for a farmer friend of Dad's, though. His wife always set her pies on the windowsill to cool, too. But they lived on the ground floor and one day one of their horses came by and ate her pies. Unfortunately, no one caught the horse in the act, so the kids got blamed . . . until it happened again! And the second time, they caught the sneaky horse!

Sometimes I wished we lived on the first floor, too. I could have used a horse to take the blame when I caused trouble—'cause I sure did plenty of that!

Homemade Pie Crust

One 10-inch deep-dish pie crust

¾ cup plus 2 tablespoons
    all-vegetable shortening
6 tablespoons boiling water

2 teaspoons milk
2¼ cups all-purpose flour
1 teaspoon salt

In a medium-sized bowl, whisk the shortening, water, and milk until the mixture has the consistency of whipped cream. Add the flour and salt and stir with a spoon until the dough forms a ball. Divide the dough into 2 equal-sized balls. Place 1 ball between 2 sheets of waxed paper; with a rolling pin, roll out to a circle slightly larger than a 10-inch deep-dish pie plate. Place in the pie plate. Pour the filling of your choice into the shell. Roll out the second dough ball to the same size and place over the filling; seal by pinching the edges together. Using a sharp paring knife, cut 6 small slits in the center of the pie top to allow steam to escape while baking. Bake according to the filling directions, or until the crust is golden.

NOTE: If you want to, you can make two 9-inch pie crusts with this recipe—in regular (not deep-dish) 9-inch pie plates.

DESSERTS

Traditional Apple Pie

about 8 servings

8 medium-sized baking apples (see Note), peeled, cored, and cut into quarters
½ cup sugar
2 tablespoons butter, cut into small pieces

1 teaspoon ground cinnamon
1 teaspoon quick-cooking tapioca
1 Homemade Pie Crust (page 60)

Preheat the oven to 425°F. In a large bowl, stir together all the ingredients except the pie crust; toss to coat the apples well. Pour the apple mixture into the pie shell; place the second circle of dough over the filling, as directed, and seal by pinching the edges together. Using a sharp paring knife, cut 6 small slits in the center of the pie top to allow steam to escape while baking. Bake for 40 to 45 minutes, or until the filling is bubbling and the crust is golden.

NOTE: Refer to the Apple Guide (page 25) for the best kinds of apples to use in pie. For a golden top that looks truly old-fashioned (like my mom's), brush the top crust with 2 teaspoons milk and sprinkle with 1 teaspoon sugar before baking.

Weren't we cute?! This is my friend Ann Osganian (now Vartigian) and me, dressed up for our annual "Baby Day" at Troy High. We had so much fun!

You can see beautiful downtown Troy behind us in the photo. Troy had everything . . . or at least we thought so back then. Oh, what great bakeries! Once in a while I'd join my friends after school for Italian pastries. My favorites were crisp, flaky pastry squares covered with powdered sugar. I remember that with just one bite my "Baby Day" costume was covered with a layer of white powder! Here's my version of the recipe that's easy enough to make at home. No, you don't have to dress like a baby to enjoy them!

Weren't we cute?!

Italian Pastry Squares

about 4 dozen pastries

¾ cup granulated sugar
½ cup water
½ cup (1 stick) butter
1 egg, beaten

1 teaspoon vanilla extract
3¾ cups all-purpose flour
Vegetable oil for frying
About ½ cup confectioners' sugar

In a medium-sized saucepan, combine the sugar, water, and butter over high heat until the butter melts. Remove from the heat and allow to cool until lukewarm. Add the egg and vanilla; mix well. Place the mixture in a large bowl and gradually mix in the flour until well combined. Roll the dough out on a lightly floured surface until paper-thin. Cut into 3-inch squares. Put 2 inches of oil in a soup pot and heat over medium heat until very hot but not smoking. Place 5 to 7 pieces of dough in the hot oil and cook for 30 to 40 seconds, or until golden on both sides, turning halfway through the cooking. Drain on paper towels. Sprinkle with confectioners' sugar; repeat with the remaining dough, and serve immediately.

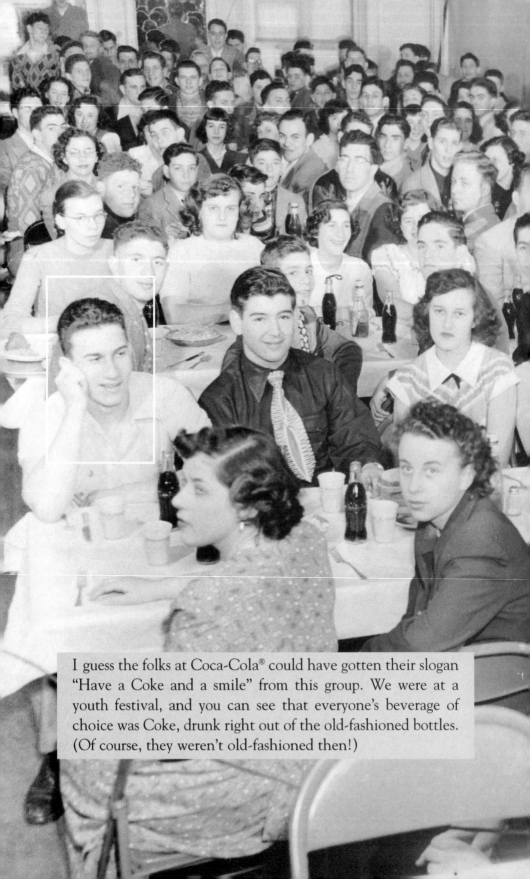

I guess the folks at Coca-Cola® could have gotten their slogan "Have a Coke and a smile" from this group. We were at a youth festival, and you can see that everyone's beverage of choice was Coke, drunk right out of the old-fashioned bottles. (Of course, they weren't old-fashioned then!)

I remember the first time I got a weekly allowance. It was a whole 25¢. My folks thought I'd save it, but I had other plans. I went right out and bought 2 nickel bottles of Coke and 2 nickel candy bars. Boy, were my parents annoyed when I came home with just 5¢! I guess I wasn't too disciplined in those days.

Later on, when I heard about cooking with cola, I thought it sounded crazy, but I gave it a try. It really makes food taste great! Let me share this favorite recipe with you.

CHICKEN

Casserole-Barbecued Chicken

4 to 6 servings

⅓ cup all-purpose flour, divided
3 teaspoons salt, divided
One 2½- to 3-pound chicken,
    cut into 8 pieces
⅓ cup vegetable oil
2 celery stalks, finely chopped
½ of a medium-sized onion,
    finely chopped

½ of a medium-sized green
    bell pepper, finely chopped
1 cup ketchup
1 cup Coca-Cola®
2 tablespoons Worcestershire sauce
½ teaspoon dried basil
½ teaspoon chili powder
⅛ teaspoon black pepper

Preheat the oven to 350°F. In a shallow dish, combine 2 tablespoons flour and 2 teaspoons salt. Rinse the chicken pieces and pat dry. Coat the chicken pieces in the flour mixture and set aside. In a large skillet, heat the oil over medium-high heat. Brown the chicken for 10 to 15 minutes, or until golden and crisp, turning once. Place in a 9" × 13" baking dish that has been coated with nonstick vegetable spray. In a large bowl, combine the remaining ingredients, including the remaining flour and 1 teaspoon salt; mix well. Spoon evenly over the chicken. Cover tightly with aluminum foil and bake for 60 to 70 minutes, or until no pink remains and the juices run clear.

NOTE: I like to serve the chicken on a bed of cooked rice, topped with the cooking juices.

Boy, did I have a great bunch of friends! Oh, the crazy times we shared. I'll never forget the time Marv Glazier and I went to New York City for the day by ourselves. It was 3 hours of laughing and fun on that train that took us from safe little Troy to that completely different world of New York. You should have seen our faces as we made our way out of the station and onto the streets! We figured we could have fit all of Troy inside Grand Central Station!

Everything was so big, and there were so many people . . . and restaurants! We had heard about a place close to the train station called the Horn & Hardart Automat. We found it without too much trouble and our jaws dropped when we walked in. It was like no place we'd ever seen. It was really neat—it had long walls lined with cubbyholes filled with food. You had to put coins in a slot by whatever item you wanted, then you could open the door and take out your food.

My favorite section was the desserts, because of the coconut cream pie. You can bet that on every trip to New York after that, I made my pilgrimage to the Automat to drop in my nickels for a piece of that dreamy cream pie.

Automat-Style Coconut Cream Pie

6 to 8 servings

1 egg yolk
⅓ cup sugar
¼ cup all-purpose flour
¼ teaspoon salt
2 cups milk
1 tablespoon butter

1 teaspoon vanilla extract
1½ cups shredded coconut
One 9-inch prepared graham
    cracker pie crust
2 cups frozen whipped topping,
    thawed

In a medium-sized bowl, mix the egg yolk, sugar, flour, and salt with a spoon; set aside. In a medium-sized saucepan, heat the milk over medium-high heat until hot; do not boil. Slowly add ½ cup of the heated milk to the sugar mixture; mix well. Slowly add the sugar mixture to the remaining milk in the saucepan; reduce the heat to medium-low and cook until thickened, stirring constantly. Add the butter and vanilla; stir until the butter melts. Remove from the heat and stir in the coconut. Pour into the pie crust. Chill for at least 2 hours, or until set. Top with the whipped topping just before serving.

NOTE: If desired, top the pie with 2 tablespoons toasted coconut. To toast shredded coconut, spread it on a rimmed baking sheet and bake in a preheated 350°F. oven for 3 to 5 minutes, until golden. Watch carefully so it doesn't burn.

Say the word *fraternity* and some people think of wild parties, lots of drinking, and the movie *Animal House*. Well, it wasn't like that when I was young. I belonged to Alpha Beta Gamma fraternity. We called it ABG and it brought together a great group of guys from the Tri-City area (that's Albany, Troy, and Schenectady, New York). We did community projects and took trips to meet with guys in other chapters around the Northeast.

Here we are in the late '40s, and again at a reunion quite a few years later. Didn't I age nicely? All of us had a lot of fun together, but, other than the friendships I made, I think the best part of ABG was that it forced me to speak in front of a crowd. You see, at the end of every meeting, each of us would have to stand up and address the whole chapter. It didn't matter so much what we talked about, as long as we made the most of communicating to a group of people. We called those speeches "good and welfare," and today I credit those experiences for getting me started in the direction of performing.

Didn't I age nicely?

I've watched loads of new food products come into the market-place over the years. Fads, desire for convenience, and ever-changing growing and transportation methods have all contributed to the creation of new food items.

Take M&M's® candies, for example. When I was a kid, many stores would carry chocolate only in the cooler months, since air-conditioning was almost unheard of and the chocolate would melt unless the store was cool. M&M's® were created to overcome that problem. Their chocolate centers were covered by a colorful sugary coating that helped them stand up to heat. That meant that I could take them to baseball games without them melting in my pocket. The success achieved in keeping these candies from melting meant that the military could supply them to our soldiers. They were stored in a tube that made them a convenient way to satisfy a sweet tooth almost anywhere.

In later years, we made these cookies with our kids. M&M's® became special to them, too! How 'bout giving them a try at *your* house?

"M&M's"® Chocolate Candies, circa 1940 - 1950.
"M&M's"® Chocolate Candies is a registered trademark of Mars, Incorporated.

Polka Dot Peanut Butter Jumbos

about 3 dozen cookies

1 cup (2 sticks) margarine or butter, softened
1 cup creamy peanut butter
1 cup granulated sugar
1 cup firmly packed light brown sugar

2 eggs
2 cups all-purpose flour
1 teaspoon baking soda
1½ cups M&M's® plain or peanut chocolate candies

Preheat the oven to 350°F. In a large bowl, with an electric beater, beat together the butter, peanut butter, and sugars until fluffy; blend in the eggs. In a medium-sized bowl, combine the flour and baking soda; add to the peanut butter mixture and mix well. Stir in the M&Ms® chocolate candies. Drop by heaping tablespoonfuls 2 inches apart onto baking sheets that have been coated with nonstick baking spray. Bake for 14 to 17 minutes, until the edges are golden brown. Allow to cool on the baking sheets for 3 minutes, then remove to a wire rack to cool completely.

If you thought I was trouble on the football team, you should have seen me in the Reserves! The Naval Reserves, that is.

I was very lucky to stay out of the fighting during my naval tour of duty. I actually enjoyed my time on the USS *Oglethorpe*. I met guys from all around the country, and we traveled the world together laughing, crying, and building great relationships.

Believe it or not, my most vivid memory of these days is of a time when we'd been out to sea for weeks without fresh provisions. A buddy of mine from Troy was the Chief Communications Officer, but he was also a wizard in the ship's galley. His specialty was desserts, so after we got hold of some fresh milk from a stop we made, Mike got out a 30-quart mixing bowl to make us a huge batch of chocolate pudding. When it was done, he and another officer were carrying the pudding to a cooler below deck. Well, the officer went down the hatch first and Mike got ready to hand down the bowl of pudding. Sounds simple, right? Well, Mike let go just a little too soon and the pudding dumped all over the officer below and dripped from every rung of the ladder!

Looking at that chocolate-covered officer, we didn't know whether to laugh or cry. I guess you'd call that bittersweet.

Needless to say, Mike and that officer became the least popular guys on that ship. The officer took a long, hot shower, Mike almost got demoted, and afterward we all had a good laugh.

As you make this homemade pudding, share a chuckle with me and **BE CAREFUL** putting it in the fridge. We wouldn't want a repeat of the ship incident.

Galley Chocolate Pudding

4 to 6 servings

⅔ cup sugar
¼ cup unsweetened cocoa
3 tablespoons cornstarch

¼ teaspoon salt
2¼ cups cold milk
1 teaspoon vanilla extract

In a medium-sized saucepan, combine the sugar, cocoa, cornstarch, and salt. Gradually stir in the milk. Bring to a boil over medium heat, stirring constantly. Remove from the heat and stir in the vanilla. Spoon into 4 to 6 individual serving dishes or 1 large bowl and refrigerate for 2 to 3 hours, or until set.

NOTE: For a down-home taste, I like to eat this pudding warm, topped with a little ice-cold milk. But for a really elegant look, it's easy to top it with fresh whipped cream or whipped topping and chocolate curls. To make chocolate curls: Use a vegetable peeler to "peel" a thick 5- to 7-ounce chocolate candy bar over the whipped cream.

When I got home from my stint in the navy,
I must have been ready to settle down. . . .

THE NEWLYWED CHALLENGE

 When I got home from my stint in the navy, I must have been ready to settle down, although I didn't know it till I met Ethel. Yup, I went on a blind date with Ethel Stillman from Albany, and I fell for her, a quiet classical pianist who sure could tickle the ivories . . . but who couldn't boil water!

That's where Mom and Flo came to the rescue. Since my love for food wasn't going to disappear, they had to jump in and teach Ethel how to cook. And she became an A+ student, making family favorites and trying out new recipes once in a while, too. Of course, not every dish was a winner, but Ethel persisted and, with each success, she experimented a bit more. Little did we know in those days that she'd go from making these cheese pancakes and cauliflower pancakes to heading up the kitchen for our own catering business!

HODGEPODGE

Cheese Pancakes

about 4 dozen pancakes

1 package (8 ounces)
   cream cheese, softened
1 cup cottage cheese
8 eggs
1 cup plain dry bread crumbs

1½ teaspoons butter, melted
¼ teaspoon black pepper
1 tablespoon sugar
About ½ cup (1 stick) butter

In a large bowl, with an electric beater on medium speed, combine the cream cheese and cottage cheese; add the eggs and continue beating until well mixed. Slowly stir in the remaining ingredients except the ½ cup butter, and let sit for 10 minutes so the bread crumbs absorb the liquid. Melt 2 tablespoons butter in a large skillet over medium-low heat. Spoon the batter by tablespoonfuls into the skillet and fry for 4 to 6 minutes, until browned on both sides, turning halfway through the frying. Remove to a rimmed baking sheet and place in a 200°F. oven to keep warm. Repeat with the remaining butter and batter. Serve immediately.

NOTE: I used to top these with real maple syrup, while my sister sprinkled hers with confectioners' sugar.

Cauliflower Pancakes

about 3 dozen pancakes

1 large head cauliflower, trimmed
and cut into florets
1½ teaspoons salt, divided
¼ cup plus 2 tablespoons vegetable
oil, divided, plus extra
if needed

1 large onion, finely chopped
6 tablespoons plain dry bread
crumbs
2 eggs, beaten
½ teaspoon garlic powder
⅛ teaspoon black pepper

Place the cauliflower in a large saucepan and add just enough water to cover; add 1 teaspoon salt to the water. Bring the water to a boil over high heat and cook, uncovered, for 20 to 25 minutes, or until the cauliflower is very tender. Meanwhile, in a large skillet, heat 2 tablespoons oil over medium-low heat and sauté the onion for 10 minutes, until golden brown; remove from the heat and set aside. Using a colander, thoroughly drain the cauliflower. In a medium-sized bowl, with a potato masher or a fork, mash the cauliflower until only small pieces remain. Add the bread crumbs, eggs, the sautéed onions, the garlic powder, the remaining ½ teaspoon salt, and the pepper; mix well. In a large skillet, heat the remaining ¼ cup oil over medium heat. Pick up 1 heaping tablespoon of the cauliflower mixture, press to form a pancake about ½ inch thick, and carefully place in the hot oil. Repeat to make 4 to 6 more pancakes, and cook for 6 minutes, or until brown on both sides, turning halfway through the cooking and adding more oil as necessary. Drain on paper towels and continue making pancakes. Serve immediately, or keep in a warm oven until ready to serve.

Typical newlyweds we were—learning to live together, finding each other's good and bad habits, realizing that we were responsible for our own lives. I was working with Dad in the butcher shop and Ethel was giving piano lessons at her parents' house. She made about $20 a week teaching. And that was pretty darned good for 1954.

We ate dinner together every night, at home, at my parents' (we lived in an apartment just downstairs from them), or at Ethel's parents'. On the nights that we ate at home and wanted a break from meat, I'd bring home some fresh fish from a local vendor. I showed Ethel how easy it was to make fish with this and other recipes, and she was amazed! We still make this scampi today, or should I say that Ethel usually makes it herself now.

Fish Scampi

6 to 8 servings

2½ pounds fresh or frozen white-fleshed fish fillets, such as cod, haddock, or whiting, thawed if frozen, cut into 2-inch chunks
1 cup (2 sticks) butter
4 garlic cloves, minced

2 scallions, minced
1 tablespoon chopped fresh parsley
1 teaspoon dried dillweed
½ teaspoon dried oregano
½ teaspoon black pepper

Preheat the oven to 350°F. Place the fish in a 9" × 13" baking dish and set aside. In a small saucepan, melt the butter over low heat and add the garlic, scallions, parsley, dillweed, oregano, and pepper. Cook for 2 minutes, stirring occasionally. Pour over the fish and bake for 20 to 25 minutes, until the fish flakes easily with a fork.

Talk about going into marriage with
your eyes closed. . . .

Talk about going into marriage with your eyes closed. . . . This photo of me with Ethel's family says it all! Who could have known then that living with me would turn the musically gifted Ethel into the kitchen talent not only for our growing family, but also for a successful catering business.

In the early days, it wasn't unusual for our meals to focus around the leftovers that I brought home from the butcher shop, just as Mom's meals had done for years. But you should have seen the look on my bride's face when I brought home an odd-shaped steak that was 2 inches thick at one end and ½ inch thick at the other. My mom was the best coach for Ethel, since she was so experienced *and* understanding. There was one time when they were making a pot roast and, instead of sprinkling on some paprika, Ethel accidentally grabbed the cinnamon. They added some other flavorings and guess what—it was a hit! Since then, we've found that some of the best recipes result from accidents. This one's meant to be made and served with love—I know Ethel's always was.

Newlyweds' Pot Roast

4 to 6 servings

¼ cup vegetable oil
One 2½-pound boneless lean beef
    chuck steak
¼ cup chopped onion
1¾ cups water

⅓ cup lemon juice
¼ cup firmly packed dark brown
    sugar
1 teaspoon salt
¼ teaspoon ground cinnamon

In a soup pot, heat the oil over medium heat. Add the steak and onions and cook for about 10 minutes, until the steak and onions are well browned, turning halfway through the cooking. Add the remaining ingredients and bring to a boil. Reduce the heat to low and simmer for 2 hours, or until the meat is fork-tender, turning occasionally. Remove the meat to a cutting board and cut into thick serving-sized slices. Serve with the cooking liquid.

The '50s were upbeat years. Men were home from the war, rock 'n' roll became popular, and all types of newfangled kitchen appliances were appearing to make women's kitchen work easier. And men were cooking, too—backyard cooking, that is. Steaks, chops, and burgers were really "in," and so was shish kebab and anything skewered.

This new fad was ideal for our family, since it was a super way to use up all the extra scraps of beef, lamb, and veal that we had at the butcher shop. Fancy grills? No way! Just the food cooked on a grate over charcoal in a kettle or in a barrel that had been cut in half. They did the job. I still love to grill. Unfortunately, back then I didn't have a chef's hat and apron to help me look the part!

Shish Kebab

6 servings

6 wooden or metal skewers
½ cup Worcestershire sauce
2 tablespoons vegetable oil
½ teaspoon onion powder
½ teaspoon garlic powder
⅛ teaspoon black pepper
1½ pounds beef top round, cut into
1½-inch cubes (about 24 cubes)

1 medium-sized yellow squash,
seeded and cut into 12 chunks
(see Note)
1 medium-sized bell pepper (any
color), cut into 12 chunks

If using wooden skewers, soak in water for 15 to 20 minutes. In a large bowl, combine the Worcestershire sauce, vegetable oil, onion powder, garlic powder, and black pepper; mix well. Add the beef and toss to coat. Cover and marinate in the refrigerator for 30 minutes. Preheat the grill to medium-high heat. Thread the beef and vegetables alternately onto the skewers so that there are 4 pieces of meat, 2 chunks of squash, and 2 chunks of peppers on each skewer. Grill for 10 to 12 minutes, or until the beef is cooked to desired doneness beyond that, turning to cook on all sides and basting with the remaining marinade for **only the first 6 to 8 minutes of grilling**. Discard any excess marinade.

NOTE: An easy way to seed the squash is to cut it in half and scrape out all the seeds at one time. Then, cut into chunks.

The honeymoon continued. . . . We were both working hard and thinking of starting a family. Back then, it was rare that we could afford to go out for dinner, but when we did, we almost always chose a diner. We loved the jukebox selectors at each booth, all the stainless steel and colorful neon, and the big plastic-coated menus. Even though there were lots of choices, I always seemed to order the same thing: meat loaf with mashed potatoes and gravy.

Diner meat loaf was different from Mom's and Ethel's. It had hard-boiled eggs in the center. At first I couldn't figure out how they got the eggs in there, but after a little experimentation, Ethel figured it out all by herself. Boy, was I surprised when she served it to me at home! I have a feeling that the novelty of eating at a diner started when we stopped at this place on our way to Washington, D.C., for our honeymoon.

Old-fashioned Meat Loaf

4 to 6 servings

1½ pounds ground beef
2 eggs, slightly beaten
½ cup plain dry bread crumbs
½ cup spaghetti sauce
½ cup water
½ of a small onion, finely minced

½ of a small green bell pepper,
  finely minced
2 garlic cloves, minced
¾ teaspoon salt
½ teaspoon black pepper
4 hard-boiled eggs

Preheat the oven to 375°F. In a large bowl, combine all the ingredients except the hard-boiled eggs; mix until thoroughly combined. Place half of the mixture in a 9" × 5" loaf pan that has been coated with nonstick vegetable spray. Place the hard-boiled eggs end to end in a lengthwise row down the center of the mixture. Place the remaining meat mixture on top, pressing down gently to seal. Bake for 50 to 60 minutes, or until no pink remains and the juices run clear. Remove from the oven, drain off the liquid, and cool for 10 minutes before slicing and serving.

Convenience foods continued to flourish. We were all infatuated with the new packaged foods we were finding in our grocery stores. Many of the food manufacturers were even supplying recipes along with the products, promoting new ways of cooking. One of the foods I remember in particular is packaged onion soup mix. We could just add water and have soup. It could be a gravy starter. And we loved mixing it with sour cream to get an easy dip. The first time we did that, we dipped anything and everything in it—crackers, bread, potato chips, vegetables, even our fingers! Onion soup mix was versatile and tasted great to us then, so it's not hard to see why it's still popular today.

Lipton® California Onion Dip

about 2 cups

1 container (16 ounces) sour cream

1 envelope (1 ounce) Lipton® onion soup mix

In a small bowl, combine the sour cream and onion soup mix; stir until thoroughly combined. Cover and chill for at least 2 hours, or until ready to serve.

LIPTON IS A REGISTERED TRADEMARK OF THOMAS J. LIPTON COMPANY

Spunky Onion Gravy

about 3 cups

3 cups water, divided
1 envelope (1 ounce) Lipton®
  onion soup mix

2 tablespoons all-purpose flour

In a small saucepan, bring 2½ cups water to a boil over medium-high heat. Stir in the onion soup mix; cover and reduce the heat to low. Simmer for 10 minutes, or until the onions are plump and tender. In a small bowl, combine the flour and the remaining ½ cup water; whisk until smooth. Increase the heat to medium-high and add the flour mixture to the onion mixture; bring to a boil. Boil for 2 minutes. Serve immediately.

NOTE: For a thicker gravy, add an additional tablespoon of flour.

Onion Brisket

4 to 6 servings

One 3- to 3½-pound beef brisket
1 large onion, coarsely chopped
1 cup ketchup

½ cup water
1 envelope (1 ounce) Lipton®
  onion soup mix

Preheat the oven to 350°F. Place the brisket in a roasting pan that has been lined with aluminum foil and coated with nonstick vegetable spray. In a medium-sized bowl, combine the remaining ingredients; mix well. Pour over the brisket and cover tightly with aluminum foil. Bake for 2½ to 3 hours, or until fork-tender.

Things changed so much in some ways, and so little in others. I carried on my dad's tradition of bringing home bushels of this or that vegetable or fruit. Ethel couldn't believe how much produce I'd bring home at one time—like the time I brought home a bushel of green peppers, and she shrieked, "What am I supposed to do with a bushel of green peppers?!"

Okay, maybe that was a bit excessive, but I was just doing what my dad had always done. So, to answer Ethel's question, I took the peppers into the kitchen, rolled up my sleeves, and went to work cutting pepper rings. Then I mixed up a few batches of my mom's onion ring batter and proceeded to dip and fry (for quite a while)! I sure was lucky that they turned out great, 'cause I didn't want to have to tell Ethel that I'd never done that before. It really is a yummy way to use up a load of peppers . . . without having your wife throw them—and you—out of the house!

French-Fried Pepper Rings

4 to 5 servings

4 medium-sized green or red bell peppers (or a combination)	½ cup all-purpose flour
Vegetable oil for frying	1 tablespoon cornstarch
¾ cup milk	¾ teaspoon baking powder
	¼ teaspoon salt

Slice the tops off the peppers and remove the seeds; cut each pepper into ¼-inch rings. Place 1 inch of oil in a soup pot and heat over medium-high heat until hot but not smoking. Meanwhile, in a medium-sized bowl, with an electric beater on medium speed, beat the remaining ingredients until smooth. Dip a few pepper rings into the batter, allowing the excess batter to drip back into the bowl. Reduce the oil to medium heat and carefully place the rings in the oil, one at a time; fry for 2 to 3 minutes, until golden, turning halfway through the cooking. Drain on paper towels. Continue until the remaining pepper rings are fried. Serve immediately, or keep warm in a 200°F. oven until ready to serve.

In the late '50s, it was common for us to invite a few couples over to our apartment to play mah-jong. It was inexpensive entertainment, and everyone usually brought something for the group to munch on. Ethel, my budding kitchen whiz, was always applauded for her sour cream coffee cake. Until then, I hadn't been a big coffee cake fan. But this one converted me. That's why Ethel usually made two at a time. One would be for the gang, the other for us.

DESSERTS

Sour Cream Coffee Cake

12 to 14 servings

1¼ cups sugar, divided
½ cup (1 stick) butter, softened
2 eggs
2 cups all-purpose flour
1 teaspoon baking powder
1 teaspoon baking soda
⅛ teaspoon salt
1 cup sour cream
2 teaspoons vanilla extract
½ cup chopped pecans
¾ teaspoon ground cinnamon

Preheat the oven to 350°F. In a large bowl, with a spoon, cream 1 cup of the sugar and the butter; add the eggs one at a time and beat (with the spoon) until well combined. Stir in the flour, baking powder, baking soda, and salt. Add the sour cream and vanilla; mix well. In a small bowl, combine the pecans, cinnamon, and the remaining ¼ cup sugar. Pour half the batter into a 10-inch tube pan that has been coated with nonstick baking spray. Top with half the pecan mixture, then spoon the rest of the batter over the pecans. Sprinkle the remaining pecan mixture over the top. Bake for 40 to 45 minutes, or until a wooden toothpick inserted in the center comes out clean. Remove from the oven and cool completely in the pan on a wire rack. Invert onto a plate to remove the cake from the pan, then invert onto a serving platter so the crumb topping is on top.

My navy years spent in the Caribbean instilled in me a love of the tropics, and a taste for tropical food. Unfortunately, when I got home, the produce sections of Troy's grocery stores didn't offer the selection they do today. Fresh pineapple was seasonal. Kiwi . . . ? Who knew what those were? Fresh coconuts were a very rare sight. The season for local fruit was extremely short. That left us with canned fruit a good deal of the time.

Canned pineapple was big in our house. Ethel bought it crushed, chunked, and in rings. Then, when she found this recipe, I had a whole new way to enjoy pineapple. After all, I've always been a kid at heart. So, what was better than a big plate of pineapple cookies with a tall glass of ice-cold milk?

Pineapple Drop Cookies

about 4 dozen cookies

3½ cups all-purpose flour
1 teaspoon baking soda
1 teaspoon salt
1½ cups sugar
1 cup vegetable shortening
2 eggs, beaten

1 teaspoon lemon juice
1 teaspoon vanilla extract
1 can (8 ounces) crushed
   pineapple in its own juice,
   undrained

Preheat the oven to 350°F. In a medium-sized bowl, combine the flour, baking soda, and salt; set aside. In a large bowl, with an electric beater on medium speed, cream the sugar and shortening until light and fluffy. Add the eggs, lemon juice, and vanilla and continue beating until combined. Reduce the speed to low and add the crushed pineapple and juice, beating until combined; gradually add the flour mixture and continue beating at low speed until thoroughly combined. (The mixture will be thick.) Drop by heaping teaspoonfuls 1 inch apart onto ungreased cookie sheets and bake for 12 to 15 minutes, or until golden. Remove to wire racks and allow to cool.

Mom and Flo broke Ethel in gradually, but one thing she had to learn about quickly was our family's traditional holiday foods. And making homemade horseradish was quite a way to be broken in! Ethel's family had always bought it already made. Not mine!

She'll surely never forget the day she first joined my mom outside to grate fresh horseradish root by hand. Homemade horseradish tastes great, but grating the root creates a powerful odor and fumes that can really sting your eyes. It was a new experience for Ethel, but I can't say an eye-opening one!

There really isn't anything that compares to fresh homemade horseradish. And now Ethel says, "Thank goodness for food processors!"

Homemade Horseradish

about 2 cups

1 to 1¼ pounds fresh horseradish
    root, peeled and grated
    (about 2 cups)

1¼ cups white vinegar
1¼ teaspoons salt
½ teaspoon sugar

Place the grated horseradish in a medium-sized bowl and add the vinegar, salt, and sugar; mix well. Place in an airtight glass container, cover, and chill until ready to use.

NOTE: My mom grated her horseradish by hand, but today I use a food processor—it makes grating a snap! Horseradish shouldn't come in contact with plastic, metal, or wood for an extended period of time. And while it packs a punch when it's first grated, it loses intensity quickly if left uncovered.

No holiday would be complete without lots of baking. The first time I found my wife baking a sponge cake, I laughed uncontrollably. She wanted to know what was so funny about what she was doing. And I told her that I'd had a flashback of my mom making a sponge cake when I was very young.

Mom would tell us to tiptoe around the house so that the cake wouldn't collapse while it was baking. At first I was annoyed, but after that, I looked on the bright side, because I realized that it was the one time that Mom couldn't get mad at me. She knew if she yelled or tried to give me a swat, she'd risk losing her precious sponge cake.

As I told Ethel this story, and continued to laugh hysterically, I realized that Ethel was close to tears, thinking that I was ruining *her* cake right then and there. Oh well, I left her to her baking as I tiptoed out of the kitchen with my fingers crossed.

Holiday Sponge Cake

12 to 14 servings

6 eggs, separated
1 cup sugar, divided
1 tablespoon grated lemon zest
1 tablespoon lemon juice
1 cup all-purpose flour

Preheat the oven to 325°F. In a large bowl, with an electric beater on medium speed, beat the egg yolks for 1 minute. Add ½ cup sugar, a tablespoon at a time, and continue beating until thickened. Add the lemon zest and lemon juice; mix well. With a rubber spatula, fold in the flour ⅓ cup at a time and set aside. In a medium-sized bowl, with an electric beater on medium speed, beat the egg whites until foamy and loose peaks form. Add the remaining ½ cup sugar, a tablespoon at a time, and continue beating until stiff peaks form. Gently fold into the egg yolk mixture. Pour the batter into an ungreased 10-inch tube pan that has been lined on the bottom with waxed paper. Bake for 1 hour, or until the top is golden and springs back when lightly touched. Invert the pan on a wire rack for at least 1 hour to cool completely, then remove from the pan and serve.

Besides all the matzo ball soup, roast brisket, and cakes we'd have for holidays, we would always have a dish we called fruit compote. It's dried fruit that has been soaked in water, then cooked. We still make it for holidays today. It's a tradition . . . a delicious one.

Fruit Compote

14 to 16 servings

3½ to 4 pounds mixed dried fruit, such as prunes, apricots, apples, and figs
1 lemon, washed, cut into quarters, seeds removed
3 cups orange juice
2 cups water
1 cup sugar
2 teaspoons ground cinnamon

Combine all the ingredients in a soup pot; mix well. Bring to a boil over high heat. Reduce the heat to low and simmer for 1½ hours, stirring occasionally, or until the fruit is very tender. Serve warm, or allow to cool, then cover and chill for at least 2 hours before serving.

I've always admitted to being a kid at heart. I'd like to think that what (or *the way*) I've eaten has kept me young. When Ethel and I were first married, she used to shake her head at me for mixing up some powdered chocolate mix, called Nestlé® Quik®, with my milk. This was popular stuff in the mid-'50s. Ethel kidded me about it until she got hooked on it, too. Soon after, our kids were drinking it, and now their kids drink it, too.

I've learned to use Nestlé Quik in my grown-up cooking, and I make these Quik Quivers™ for the kids, although I have to admit that every once in a while I still mix some into my milk and slurp up every last drop.

Quik Quivers™

about 10 Quivers

2 cups milk
½ cup Nestlé® Quik® Chocolate
   Powder

¼ cup sugar
2 envelopes (0.25 ounce each)
   unflavored gelatin

In a small saucepan, combine all the ingredients; mix well. Bring to a boil over medium-high heat, stirring until smooth. Pour into an 8-inch square baking dish and let cool at room temperature for about 30 minutes. Cover with plastic wrap and chill for 5 hours, or until firm to the touch. Use a cookie cutter or knife to cut into different shapes. Serve cold.

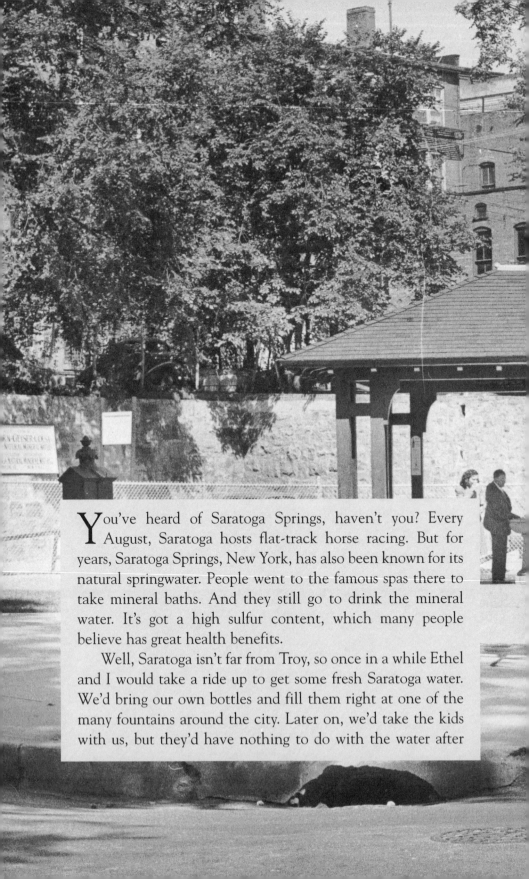

Y ou've heard of Saratoga Springs, haven't you? Every August, Saratoga hosts flat-track horse racing. But for years, Saratoga Springs, New York, has also been known for its natural springwater. People went to the famous spas there to take mineral baths. And they still go to drink the mineral water. It's got a high sulfur content, which many people believe has great health benefits.

Well, Saratoga isn't far from Troy, so once in a while Ethel and I would take a ride up to get some fresh Saratoga water. We'd bring our own bottles and fill them right at one of the many fountains around the city. Later on, we'd take the kids with us, but they'd have nothing to do with the water after

their first tastes. They think it smells and tastes like rotten eggs . . . and maybe they're right! But I grew up on it, so I'm used to it.

The first time our youngest, Chuck, tried it, the other kids set him up. They said it was really delicious, and that he'd love it. Well, my daughter, Caryl, got ready with her camera, and after Chuck came up from his sip, she caught his face in full "Yuck!" We've laughed over that for years.

Does the water really have healing powers? I don't know. But I like it, and I always enjoy going back to Saratoga for another few sips.

With the arrival of our children—first Steve,
then Caryl, then Chuck—our lives changed
as we never could have imagined.

FAMILY FUN

With the arrival of our children—first Steve, then Caryl, then Chuck—our lives changed as we never could have imagined. After all, we were practically kids ourselves! Growing together was a fun learning adventure for us all.

And, speaking of adventures, take a look at us on our first major family vacation. We drove to Washington, D.C., to visit Ethel's sister, Suzanne, who worked for the government. It was great to have our own personal tour guide. Here we are at the Capitol and at the Reflecting Pool that flows between the Lincoln Memorial and the Washington Monument. Notice our oldest's, Steve's, less-than-happy face in these shots. That was because his shoes were too tight! Boy, do kids grow quickly! Unfortunately, that's our kids' most vivid memory of that whole trip! Oh well, it gives us all a good laugh now.

On our way to Washington, Ethel and I decided to try out some new diners, since a diner had made such an impression on us when we honeymooned there. The kids don't remember, but Ethel and I sure loved the Salisbury steak we ordered. It had green beans mixed in. Now, it might not sound traditional, but it sure was a yummy way to get the kids to eat their veggies! So, the trip wasn't totally painful for Steve. . . .

Beefed-up Salisbury Steak

6 servings

1½ pounds ground beef
1 large onion, finely chopped, divided
1 can (8 ounces) cut green beans, drained and chopped
½ teaspoon paprika
¼ teaspoon garlic powder
½ teaspoon salt
½ teaspoon black pepper, divided
3 tablespoons all-purpose flour
1 can (14½ ounces) ready-to-use beef broth

In a large bowl, combine the ground beef, ½ cup onion, the green beans, paprika, garlic powder, salt, and ¼ teaspoon pepper. Mix well and form into 6 oval-shaped patties, each about ¼ inch thick. Heat a large nonstick skillet over medium-high heat. Add the patties and scatter the remaining chopped onion around them. Cook for 10 minutes, turning halfway through the cooking. In a small bowl, whisk together the flour, beef broth, and the remaining ¼ teaspoon pepper. Add to the skillet and bring to a boil. Reduce the heat to low and simmer for 5 minutes, or until the sauce thickens and no pink remains in the meat, stirring occasionally. Serve the patties topped with the sauce.

Growing kids meant more and more cooking for Ethel. She always made sure that we had well-balanced meals, and all 5 of us always sat down to a nice dinner *together*. It was our only time to unwind and catch up on what had happened each day.

Those were sparse years for us, but the kids never knew how difficult it was for Ethel and me to make ends meet. Fortunately, we found ways to stretch our dollars, especially in the kitchen. For example, since canned soups and vegetables were really popular in the '60s, it was easy and economical for us all to enjoy our favorite corn soup. It's still hard to believe what great homemade taste it has, since it goes together so quickly!

Our "cracker-box" house on Michigan Avenue.

Corn Soup

4 to 6 servings

2 cans (14¾ ounces each) cream-style corn

1⅔ cups milk

2 tablespoons butter

¼ teaspoon black pepper

In a large saucepan, combine all the ingredients over medium heat. Cook for 5 to 7 minutes, or until heated through, stirring frequently.

It's still hard to believe what great homemade taste this has, since it goes together so quickly!

Steve's favorite part was slurping in
those last stray spaghetti strands.

One thing you could count on in our kitchen was that nothing would go to waste . . . I mean nothing. Ethel sure had a way with leftovers! So, many times I'd come home from work and we'd both laugh at what she'd done to get an extra meal out of leftovers.

We found that we liked baked spaghetti so much that she started making extra spaghetti on purpose, just so we could have it baked the next day! Casseroles were big then anyway, and this one is loaded with ground beef, sautéed onions, and peppers. Steve's favorite part was slurping in those last stray spaghetti strands. All you had to do was look at his face to tell how happy he was to have leftovers. Boy, were we glad!

Baked Spaghetti

9 to 12 servings

1 package (16 ounces) spaghetti
1 pound lean ground beef
1 medium-sized onion, chopped
1 medium-sized green bell pepper, chopped

½ teaspoon salt
1 jar (26 ounces) spaghetti sauce

Preheat the oven to 350°F. Prepare the spaghetti according to the package directions; drain, rinse, drain again, and set aside in a large bowl. Meanwhile, in a large skillet, brown the ground beef over medium heat until no pink remains; drain off the excess liquid. Add the onions, peppers, and salt; cook for 6 to 8 minutes, until the vegetables are fork-tender. Stir in the spaghetti sauce. Add to the spaghetti; toss until well mixed. Pour into a 9" × 13" baking dish that has been coated with nonstick vegetable spray; cover tightly with aluminum foil and bake for 50 minutes. Remove the foil and bake for 5 to 8 minutes, until the top is crisp.

NOTE: This is the way to make it from scratch, but you can adjust the ingredients and the amounts to make a casserole with your leftover spaghetti. And I like to top it with 3 cups (12 ounces) shredded Cheddar cheese before baking to give it a different flavor and texture.

By the mid-'60s Ethel had mastered the art of "canned cooking." She could turn any pantry item into a meal. Take canned salmon. . . . Red salmon was quite inexpensive in those days (yes, less than tuna), so it was a staple in our house.

The kids loved it any way Ethel made it, but especially as salmon croquettes. It was a nourishing, quick dinner that we (especially Caryl) looked forward to. Ethel made a dill dipping sauce to go along with the croquettes, and that became Caryl's favorite sauce, dressing, dip . . . she wanted it with everything! Chuck liked the croquettes, too, because they were easy to eat with his fingers. For years the kids teased each other about what type of fish a salmon croquette was and where it could be caught. Well, they still like croquettes today, and now they have fun serving them to their own children. That makes Ethel and me *really* happy.

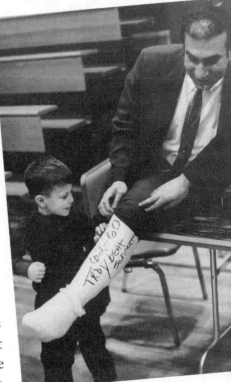

Chuck checking out Daddy's boo-boo.

Salmon Croquettes

12 croquettes

1 can (15½ ounces) pink or red
    salmon, drained, boned, and
    flaked
4 eggs, beaten
1½ cups plain dry bread crumbs,
    divided

⅓ cup finely chopped onion
1 tablespoon chopped fresh parsley
¼ teaspoon salt
⅛ teaspoon black pepper
2 to 3 tablespoons vegetable oil

In a large bowl, combine the salmon, eggs, 1 cup bread crumbs, the onion, parsley, salt, and pepper; mix well. Form the mixture into 12 oval-shaped patties, each about ¼ inch thick. Place the remaining ½ cup bread crumbs in a shallow dish and coat the patties on both sides with the bread crumbs. In a large skillet, heat 2 tablespoons oil over medium heat, and sauté the patties for 5 to 8 minutes, until golden brown, turning halfway through the cooking and adding up to 1 tablespoon more oil if necessary. Drain on paper towels, then remove to a serving platter and serve immediately.

NOTE: My kids always loved dipping each forkful into Easiest Dill Sauce.

Easiest Dill Sauce

about 1½ cups

1 cup sour cream
½ cup mayonnaise
1 tablespoon sweet pickle relish

2 teaspoons lemon juice
1 teaspoon dried dillweed

In a small bowl, combine all the ingredients; mix well. Cover and chill for at least 1 hour before serving.

NOTE: The longer the sauce is chilled, the stronger the dill flavor will be. I recommend making this the night before you plan to serve it.

Eating out was a rare treat for our family. When we did eat out, it'd be a casual meal at a little food stand—no fancy restaurants for us in those days. The kids loved the places we went, like Hot Dog Charlie's® in downtown Troy. The place had been around since 1922, and for good reason: Their hot dogs were true classics!

Charlie's hot dogs were miniature hot dogs in miniature buns covered with chopped onions (or without, for the kids) and their own chili sauce. At just 15¢ a pop you'd get a "show" with your dinner, too, since the cook would line a bunch of buns all the way up his arm. Then he'd fill them with the hot dogs and proceed to add the toppings and sauce without spilling a drop! That's why these hot dogs (which couldn't possibly be assembled the same way today) were nicknamed "hairy arms."

Hot Dog Charlie's® in downtown Troy.

I'd eat quite a few of these at a sitting, while the kids got a kick out of how small the dogs and buns were. I never did get Charlie's to share their sauce recipe with me, but we use my own version for making hot dog memories with our grandchildren these days. Full-sized or cocktail-sized, it doesn't matter. Just cook up some hot dogs, make a batch of this sauce, and grab a cold soda. You're in for a real treat.

Chili Dogs

6 to 8 servings

3 tablespoons vegetable oil, divided
¾ pound ground beef
1 medium-sized onion, finely chopped
1 tablespoon chili powder
1 tablespoon paprika
2 teaspoons dried oregano
½ teaspoon minced garlic
1 teaspoon salt
¼ teaspoon black pepper
1 pound hot dogs
6 to 8 hot dog buns, split

In a large saucepan, heat 2 tablespoons oil over medium-high heat. Add the ground beef and onions and cook for 5 to 7 minutes, or until no pink remains in the beef and the onions are tender. Reduce the heat to low and add the remaining ingredients except the hot dogs and buns; simmer for 30 minutes. Meanwhile, heat the remaining 1 tablespoon oil in a large skillet over medium-high heat and cook the hot dogs to desired doneness. Place the hot dogs in the buns and top with the ground beef mixture. Serve immediately, with any remaining ground beef mixture on the side.

To this day, if I mention Jack's Hamburgers, my kids' eyes light up! When the kids were little, all Ethel and I had to do was announce we were going to Jack's, and, in no time, they'd be piled into the Chevy station wagon (we always had one of those—a used one) and we'd be on our way out to Jack's.

Now, if you didn't know what you were looking for, you'd probably drive right by the place. It was a tiny shack that made burgers with a big taste. We'd pull up into the rocky, unpaved parking area and let the kids decide whether to have a carhop wait on us or to go right up to the window to order the burgers, then reach into the outside cooler for their individual-sized bottles of ice-cold chocolate milk. Because Chuck was so little, he had a really hard time getting his bottle. But that never stopped him!

The kids liked to watch the cook make our square burgers and top each one with a mountain of fried onions. Oh, those onions! They were cooked right in the hamburger grease, so they were indescribably tasty! (And back then, we weren't worried about how much fat we ate.)

John and Mike always made us feel welcome at Jack's. I think a lot of that had to do with my telling him I was a Brooklyn Dodgers fan (even though I wasn't!). You see, any fan of the Dodgers was a special guest at Jack's!

Smothered Onion Burgers

6 servings

¼ cup vegetable oil
4 large onions, cut into ¼-inch
    slices
1½ pounds ground beef

1 teaspoon salt
½ teaspoon black pepper
6 hamburger buns, split

In a large skillet, heat the oil and sauté the onions over medium-high heat for 20 to 25 minutes, until caramelized and crisp; remove the onions to a medium-sized bowl. Meanwhile, in another medium-sized bowl, combine the ground beef, salt, and pepper; mix well and form into six ¼-inch-thick patties. (These are thin, like many fast-food burgers.) Cook the hamburgers in the skillet over medium-high heat for 3 to 4 minutes, or until no pink remains and the juices run clear, turning halfway through the cooking. Return the onions to the skillet for 1 to 2 minutes to reheat. Place the hamburgers on the buns and smother with the onions; serve immediately.

NOTE: To make square hamburgers (like the ones I remember), line a 9" × 13" baking dish with waxed paper. Press the ground beef into the bottom of the pan and then cut into 6 thin patties.

As fast food caught on in the rest of the country, it caught on with our family, too. Sure, we had our local favorites, but if we were on our way somewhere and had to catch dinner really fast, the kids would always ask to "get a bucket." So, we'd stop off at the Kentucky Fried Chicken® restaurant in Albany for a bucket of the Colonel's Original Recipe® chicken with all the go-alongs.

Now, it wasn't a weekly ritual, by any means, but as life got busier and busier for our growing family, we kept up as best we could. And, boy, did little Chuckie (nobody's called him that in years!) love to squirt honey onto his chicken from those little packets. Of course, after we'd finish the bucket of chicken, we'd always need a bath for the kids!

PHOTOGRAPHS COURTESY OF KFC CORPORATION

115

"Watch out, world! Caryl's in business!" From the very beginning, Caryl has followed in my footsteps—from her desire to perform to her adventurous personality. So, when she marched into the house one day looking for the card table and asking to borrow an empty cigar box, nobody was too surprised. She was setting up a fresh-squeezed lemonade and Kool-Aid® stand with some kids in the neighborhood.

It didn't matter that most of the kids were older than her. She still made her opinions known when it came to discussing which corner to set up on, how much they'd charge per glass, and the other important decisions. I'll admit they did a good job! Unfortunately, we lived on a dead-end street, so they didn't get much traffic. So, of course, we parents were their best customers. Oh, well. It was a good lesson for all of them, even if they *did* drink up most of their profits!

Lemonade Base

about 2⅔ cups

½ cup water
1½ cups sugar

1½ cups fresh-squeezed lemon juice
Grated zest of 1 lemon

In a medium-sized saucepan, bring the water to a boil over medium-high heat; stir in the sugar until completely dissolved. Remove from the heat and stir in the lemon juice and zest. Let cool to room temperature. Store the lemonade base in a covered container in the refrigerator, or store in the freezer until needed; then just thaw, mix as directed below, and serve.

To make lemonade by the glass: Combine ¼ cup lemonade base, ¾ cup cold water, and ice cubes.

To make lemonade by the pitcher (about 8 cups): Combine 2⅔ cups lemonade base, 5 cups cold water, and ice cubes.

NOTE: Lemons will squeeze more easily if at room temperature or if softened in the microwave (on low for just a few seconds).

After the bawl is over . . . how to have dinner on time

Serve Swanson TV Brand Dinners

Everybody appreciates such extra good taste! And Swanson TV Brand Dinners make mealtime a breeze. Like turkey? Swanson gives you big tender slices with savory dressing and gravy, plus buttered whipped potatoes and garden peas. Delicious, of course . . . this or any of the nine Swanson varieties.

FROZEN

SWANSON

"TV" DINNERS

Made only by *Campbell* Soup Company

Only Swanson comes so close to your own home cooking

'TV' and 'TV DInner' are registered trademarks

As the popularity of television grew, so did the meals that most of our friends and our kids' friends ate in front of the TV. They were called "TV Dinners." We still insisted on eating our regular family dinners in the kitchen, with the television turned off, but if Ethel and I went out on a Saturday night, we'd give in and give the babysitter permission to let the kids eat in front of the TV.

Now, Ethel and I hadn't grown up on TV dinners, so we still preferred making our own meals. But once in a while we used the idea and turned our own leftovers into TV dinners by placing the food in compartmentalized trays and freezing them for quick meals for those times when Steve and Chuck had Little League practice, Caryl had late piano lessons, or Ethel or I had community center meetings.

Frozen dinners came in really handy, as the rest of the country had already found out! And the commercial ones have come a long way from their rather basic beginnings. You can get almost any type of food, even "light" meals, in TV dinner–style today, and they're still helping a lot of American families enjoy balanced meals in a hurry.

We loved getting out for our occasional
Saturday-night costume parties . . . and the kids
loved staying home with the sitter and TV dinners!

Our kids went to Troy's Public School #18 for every grade from kindergarten through eighth. They walked to and from school *and* walked home for lunch every day, too. It was a small school compared to today's schools, and it had no cafeteria.

By the time the kids got home for lunch, there wasn't much time to eat, so they'd have soup and sandwiches or maybe some macaroni and cheese made from a box. They loved it (Ethel, too)! Not only was it quick and tasty, but it was the first thing our kids learned to "cook" by themselves. It gave them a real feeling of satisfaction to get out the ingredients (few that there were) and mix them up themselves.

When we let them make it for weekend dinners, we'd add some ingredients to it to "dress it up." Sometimes we'd add canned or frozen peas (thawed and/or drained, of course), sometimes some leftover cooked veggies, or, my favorite, some flaked tuna. It was fun for the kids, and sometimes a big surprise for Ethel and me!

Dressed-up Macaroni and Cheese

4 to 6 servings

2 packages (7.25 ounces each) macaroni and cheese dinner
1 can (12 ounces) water-packed tuna, drained and flaked
1 cup (4 ounces) shredded Cheddar cheese

½ cup milk
1 cup sour cream
2 tablespoons chopped fresh dillweed
½ teaspoon black pepper

Preheat the oven to 350°F. Cook the macaroni according to the package directions; drain, rinse, drain again, and place in a large bowl. Add the sauce packets and the remaining ingredients; mix well. Spoon the mixture into a 2-quart casserole dish that has been coated with nonstick vegetable spray. Cover with aluminum foil and bake for 20 minutes. Uncover and bake for 10 more minutes, or until heated through.

Dinner would be over, the kids would be doing their homework or watching TV, and then it would happen—the abrupt clanging of the ice cream truck's bell would have the Lesnicks, Apples, Richtols, and our kids leaping out the front door in a flash. (Remember, we lived on a dead-end street, so it was pretty safe.)

Even if they were in the bath, they'd race into their pajamas so they wouldn't miss their favorite goodies. And if the truck happened to arrive while we were eating dinner, we'd let the kids get their treats and keep them in the freezer till after dinner.

Steve liked the strawberry shortcake on a stick, Caryl liked the sky-blue Popsicles® and the Creamsicles®, and Chuck liked just about anything. Ethel and I looked forward to the ice cream sundae cones, topped with crushed peanuts.

It never failed, Chuck would end up back in the house with his face and pj's covered with ice cream. Oh, well, Ethel just did some more of what she was famous for . . . cleaning!

Peanut Sundae Cones

12 cones

12 paper cups (5-ounce size)
1 cup chopped salted peanuts, divided
1 cup (6 ounces) semisweet chocolate chips

2 tablespoons vegetable shortening
1 quart vanilla ice cream
12 sugar cones

Place 1 teaspoon of the nuts in the bottom of each paper cup. In a medium-sized microwave-safe bowl, heat the chocolate and shortening in the microwave on high power for 1 minute. Stir until smooth and completely melted; heat for additional 10-second intervals if needed. Stir the remaining ¾ cup nuts into the melted chocolate, then spoon about 2 teaspoons of the mixture into each cup, enough to come halfway up the side of each cup. Place a scoop of ice cream in each cone and invert the cone into the cup, pressing the ice cream into the chocolate mixture. Freeze the cones (in the cups) for 3 to 4 hours. When ready to serve, just peel the paper off each ice cream cone.

August in our area always meant lots of fresh corn and other produce, warm days and warmer nights, and, of course, getting ready for a new school year. But right before school started, the kids would get their last reprieve—we'd take them to the Schaghticoke Fair. It was a local county fair that lasted for 5 days.

There were 4-H buildings full of agricultural displays, Ferris wheels, pony rides, and, of course, "fair food." There was hot popcorn, wispy, sweet cotton candy, grills full of sizzling sausage and peppers, and ice cream sundaes.

We'd walk all around the fair, then we'd always end up choosing our family favorites, crispy fried dough that we'd get right out of the deep fryer (the hotter, the better), and fresh, crunchy candy apples. And if some of the coating got stuck to the kids' teeth for a while, it didn't matter. We'd brush it out later. This was our last summer fling. Fall was coming and, with it, cooler temperatures. But we didn't dwell on those thoughts too much around Labor Day—we were busy making Fair memories that would keep us warm till spring.

State-Fair Fried Dough

30 to 35 pieces

2 cups vegetable oil
One 1-pound loaf frozen bread
    dough, thawed

½ cup sugar

In a large skillet, heat the oil over medium-high heat until very hot but not smoking. Meanwhile, pull the bread dough apart into 1-inch pieces. Test the oil for readiness by carefully placing 1 piece of dough into the pan: It is ready when bubbles appear around the edges of the dough. Add a few more pieces of dough to the oil and fry until golden brown on the bottom. Turn the dough over and brown the second side. Remove from the skillet with a slotted spoon and drain on paper towels. Repeat until all the dough is fried. Place the sugar in a shallow dish or a resealable plastic storage bag. Roll or shake the fried dough in the sugar to coat completely. Serve hot.

NOTE: BE CAREFUL making this! The oil will be very hot!

County-Fair Candy Apples

6 apples

6 wooden frozen dessert sticks
6 medium-sized red apples
   (see page 25 for suggestions)
1 teaspoon butter
3 cups sugar

⅔ cup light corn syrup
⅔ cup water
1 teaspoon white vinegar
8 drops red food color

Thoroughly wash and dry the apples. Remove the stems from the apples and place a dessert stick securely through the stem end of each apple. Grease a rimmed baking sheet with the butter and set aside. In a medium-sized saucepan, combine the sugar, corn syrup, water, vinegar, and food color over medium-high heat. Cook for 12 to 14 minutes, or until the syrup reaches the hard ball stage (see Note), or until a candy thermometer reaches 295°F. Remove from the heat and dip each apple into the syrup mixture, coating completely. **Be careful—the mixture is very hot!** Place the apples on the baking sheet to cool.

NOTE: To test for the hard ball stage, drop a teaspoon of the candy mixture from a teaspoon into a glass of cold water. If the candy mixture hardens, the mixture has reached the hard ball stage.

When I started to go back through photos and stories for this book, I realized I could have devoted a whole chapter to our family camping days. We call them the "good ol' days," but were they? Whenever we talk about our camping outings to nearby Lake George, Ethel is quick to remind us that she had to wash Chuck's diapers in a special bucket over the campfire. (We didn't have disposables in 1965.) But then we all laugh and remember the fun we had.

When we talk about those days, we can almost feel how crisp and fresh the air was, how moist and lush the woods were, and how the smell of campfires surrounded us from the moment we entered the Hearthstone campgrounds until we were on the road back home days later.

Husky Grilled Corn

6 ears

6 ears fresh corn in the husk
½ cup (1 stick) butter, melted

Salt and black pepper to taste

Place the ears of corn (still in the husks) in a large pot of cold water and soak for 1 hour. Preheat the grill to medium-high heat. Remove the corn from the water and wrap each ear (still in the husk) in a piece of heavy-duty aluminum foil. Place the wrapped corn on the grill rack and cook for 18 to 22 minutes, or until the kernels are tender. **Carefully open the foil and remove the corn, then remove the husks and silk from the corn.** Serve with the melted butter, salt, and pepper.

Campfire Home Fries

4 to 6 servings

4 pounds all-purpose potatoes
¼ cup vegetable oil
¼ cup (½ stick) butter

1 teaspoon salt
⅛ teaspoon black pepper

Place the potatoes in a large pot and add just enough water to cover them. Heat over high heat until boiling, then reduce the heat to medium and continue cooking for 30 to 35 minutes, or until fork-tender. Drain and allow to cool slightly, then cut into ¼-inch slices. In a large skillet, heat the oil and butter over high heat until the butter is melted. Add the potatoes and sprinkle with the salt and pepper. Cook for 25 to 30 minutes, until browned and crisp on both sides, turning occasionally.

My navy years paid off! I was quite the pro at pitching the tent, starting the fire, rowing the boat, and baiting the fishing hooks. We made breakfast and dinner over the campfire, and, boy, did everything taste better cooked over a campfire!

Some mornings we'd make eggs and home-fried potatoes in the big cast-iron skillet. Other days I'd make what the kids called "Dad's Special Pancakes." For dinner we'd boil a big pot of water for potatoes or roast fresh corn right in the fire. Soaking the corn, then wrapping it in foil and throwing it into the fire meant it'd come out with a rich, nutty taste from cooking with the husks on. If we hadn't had much fishing luck that day (which was usually the case), we'd grill up some hamburgers or hot dogs.

We brought lots of provisions with us, and we bought ice and anything else we needed at the closest store, about 6 miles from the campgrounds. The kids loved it all, except that if they got up in the middle of the night, we'd have to get our shoes on, grab a flashlight, and hike a bit to get to the bathrooms. But it was worth it. To this day, I think Steve and Chuck would still rather sleep outside in sleeping bags . . . if only their wives would let them!

Homemade Cinnamon Pancake Mix

about 7 cups

5 cups all-purpose flour
1¼ cups instant nonfat dry milk
    powder
⅓ cup sugar

2 tablespoons baking powder
½ teaspoon ground cinnamon
1 tablespoon salt

Combine all the ingredients in a large bowl; mix well. Place in a large airtight container, seal, and store in a cool, dry place. Use within 6 to 8 months, to make a few batches of Cinnamon Pancakes.

Cinnamon Pancakes

Ten to twelve 4-inch pancakes

1½ cups Homemade Cinnamon
    Pancake Mix
1 egg, slightly beaten

1 cup water
4 tablespoons vegetable oil,
    divided, plus extra if needed

Place the pancake mix in a medium-sized bowl. Add the egg, water, and 3 tablespoons oil; mix well and let stand for 5 minutes. Heat the remaining 1 tablespoon oil in a nonstick griddle or large skillet over medium heat. Pour ¼ cup of batter per pancake onto the griddle and cook the pancakes for about 2 minutes, or until the bottoms are brown and bubbles have appeared on top. Turn, adding additional oil if necessary, and cook for 1 to 2 minutes longer, or until browned on both sides. Serve immediately, or keep warm in a low oven until all the pancakes are cooked.

Not only did we cook up a storm on camping trips, but we cooked almost anything on our back porch, too. Summers passed quickly in Troy, so we'd make the most of the nice weather and get outside to grill, eat, and play as much as we could.

We all enjoyed our grilled breakfasts during our early camping years, so in later years I decided to make some of our home breakfasts on the grill, too. On Sunday mornings, since the kids had no Sunday school in the summer, I loved making everybody French toast. I'd put a heavy griddle top on the barbecue grill racks and make it outside. Ethel was thrilled, 'cause there was less mess to clean up in the kitchen (and I loved getting creative . . . although she called it "making a mess").

If I must say so myself, my challah French toast was fantastic! And we'd try each piece with a different topping, from a mix of cinnamon and sugar to real New York State or Vermont maple syrup (Vermont is just 20 miles from Troy), raspberry or black cherry preserves, and even fancier sauces, if Ethel had gotten a chance to make them up the day before.

Once we were living in our second house, the one where we eventually based our catering business, we'd have our summer Sunday French toast, then we'd all jump in our pool to clean off!

Challah French Toast

6 to 8 servings

7 eggs
¼ cup milk
1 teaspoon ground cinnamon
3 tablespoons butter

One 1-pound loaf egg bread (challah), cut into eight 1-inch slices

Beat the eggs in a medium-sized bowl. Add the milk and cinnamon; mix well. Melt 1 tablespoon butter in a large skillet over medium heat. Dip each bread slice in the egg mixture, then cook for 2 to 4 minutes, until golden on both sides, turning halfway through the cooking; add the remaining butter to the skillet as needed. Cut the French toast in half diagonally and serve with your favorite topping.

NOTE: My son Chuck likes this with Vanilla Butter Maple Syrup, while my other son, Steve, and my daughter, Caryl, like it with homemade Raspberry Sauce. Ethel and I started off eating it with real maple syrup, and now sometimes we simply top it with a sprinkle of confectioners' sugar. There are so many choices!!

Vanilla Butter Maple Syrup

about 1 cup

1 cup maple syrup
3 tablespoons butter

1 tablespoon vanilla extract

In a small saucepan, combine all the ingredients over medium-low heat. Cook until the butter has melted and the syrup is warmed through.

NOTE: This is a great topping for Challah French Toast, or your favorite pancakes or waffles.

Raspberry Sauce

about 2 cups

1 package (12 ounces) frozen
    raspberries
½ cup sugar

½ cup water
1 tablespoon cornstarch

In a medium-sized saucepan, combine all the ingredients over medium-low heat. Cook for 8 to 10 minutes, stirring occasionally, or until the sauce has thickened.

NOTE: I used to use this sauce just for topping Challah French Toast, until I discovered how good it is over ice cream. Now I use it as a topping for all my favorite desserts.

Mention New Year's Eve and most people think of champagne, noisemakers, and parties. Not our two youngest. Caryl and Chuck's New Year's Eve memories are rich in thoughts of food. Why? Because when they were old enough to stay home alone, and Steve would sleep over at a friend's, they'd make some kind of special food for their own New Year's Eve celebration.

Once they made fancy lemon-flavored Italian *pizzelle* cookies; they're made in a press so that they come out with a stenciled design on them. But then they discovered cheese fondue, and that became their New Year's tradition. They'd cut up chunks of Italian or French bread and slices of apples and pears, and make themselves a pot of what they thought was an incredibly cheesy dip.

After they had that, they'd quickly rip up whatever colorful paper they could find, so they could toss confetti at each other (and all over our dogs) at midnight. That was their ritual for a number of years, until Caryl started babysitting for her cousins and Chuck started staying at a friend's house, too. But they still laugh about those times. In fact, this year, just after Caryl and her family moved to Florida to join the rest of us here, they got together again to repeat the fondue tradition with their spouses and friends. This time, they even started it off with a little white wine, as in the traditional fondue recipes. Obviously, it was a tasty, fun tradition worthy of bringing back to life.

New Year's Eve Cheese Fondue

4 to 6 servings

1 garlic clove, cut in half
¾ cup dry white wine
3 cups (12 ounces) shredded
    Swiss cheese
1 tablespoon cornstarch

⅛ teaspoon ground nutmeg
¼ teaspoon salt
⅛ teaspoon black pepper
1 loaf (1 pound) French bread,
    cut into bite-sized pieces

Rub the cut sides of the garlic clove over the inside of a medium-sized saucepan, then discard the garlic. Add the wine and heat over medium-low heat until bubbly. In a medium-sized bowl, combine the cheese, corn-starch, nutmeg, salt, and pepper; toss to coat the cheese completely. Add ¼ cup of the cheese mixture to the wine, stirring constantly. Continue to add the cheese mixture by ¼-cupfuls, stirring for 3 to 5 minutes, until all the cheese is melted and the mixture is thoroughly blended. Transfer to a fondue pot or a chafing dish to keep hot. Serve immediately with the bread pieces for dipping.

NOTE: I also like to serve apple slices with this, in addition to the bread.

Snacks . . . all kids love 'em and mine were no different. Growing kids seem to be hungry all the time, especially after school. Back then there were the nursery school events (Ethel was the school chairman), bake sales, Cub Scout meetings (Ethel was a den mother), Little League baseball dinners, and marching band rehearsals. We were always baking 'cause everybody needed to bring a snack or dessert to their activity.

Well, we had our share of sweets to choose from, especially after Ethel discovered Cool Whip® whipped topping. We got one of the kids' favorite recipes from a neighbor. It was called wacky cake and used a cake mix and a lot of whipped topping. Now, we always liked fresh whipped cream, but let's face it, with three active kids, Ethel had her hands full. So, Cool Whip really helped her out.

Now that good-old-fashioned taste comes all whipped.

Around the time of our introduction to wacky cake, other cakes with similarly unusual mixing methods became popular. Some of them were made with different flavors of soda, and some with gelatin, like this poke cake.

When you watch my daily television segments today, you'll see that I'm still fascinated by these types of cakes. And many of my recipes use whipped topping because it's so easy and versatile. No, I'm not telling you to put away the heavy cream and the beaters, but I know that life has gotten more complicated than ever, and we should use whatever help we can find.

Wacky Cake

12 to 15 servings

3 cups all-purpose flour
2 cups sugar
⅔ cup unsweetened cocoa
2 teaspoons baking soda
½ teaspoon salt
2 teaspoons vanilla extract

4 teaspoons white vinegar
1⅓ cups vegetable oil
3 eggs
2 cups water
Frozen whipped topping, thawed,
    for garnish

Preheat the oven to 350°F. In a 9" × 13" baking pan, stir together the flour, sugar, cocoa, baking soda, and salt. With a spoon, make 3 evenly spaced wells in the mixture. Pour the vanilla in the first well, the vinegar in the second, and the oil in the third. Break an egg over each well and pour the water over the entire mixture. Mix well and bake for 40 to 45 minutes, or until a wooden toothpick inserted in the center comes out clean. Cool in the pan on a wire rack, then cut and serve, topped with dollops of whipped topping.

Gelatin Poke Cake

12 to 15 servings

1 package (18.5 ounces) white
    cake mix
1 box (4-serving size) strawberry-
    flavored gelatin

1 cup boiling water
½ cup cold water
1 container (8 ounces) frozen
    whipped topping, thawed

Preheat the oven to 350°F. Prepare the cake mix according to the package directions and bake in a 9" × 13" baking dish that has been coated with nonstick baking spray; let cool for 15 minutes. Pierce the cake all over at ½-inch intervals with a 2-pronged carving fork. In a small bowl, combine the gelatin and boiling water; stir until the gelatin is completely dissolved. Stir in the cold water and carefully pour the gelatin mixture over the top of the cake. Cover and chill for 3 to 4 hours. Frost with the whipped topping, cut, and serve.

Almost everyone who grew up in New York's Capital District area at any time from the early 1900s to the 1960s was familiar with the Freihofer's® Bakery delivery truck. Freihofer's Bakery was started by the Freihofer family, originally from Philadelphia, to provide fresh bread, and then sweet baked goods, also, for working women. There were so many of those in the "Collar City," as Troy was known, because of its bustling shirt-and-collar-making industry around the turn of the century.

Their first home deliveries were made by horse and wagon, then later, when our kids were growing up, deliveries were made by truck. We'd put our yellow cardboard sign, with the Freihofer's name written across it in black script, in our front window if we wanted the delivery man to stop at our house.

Oh, what wonderful things they made! To this day, authentic Freihofer's chocolate chip cookies are sought after by people around the country who, at one time or another, have experienced that homemade flavor that has come to represent the Capital District. Our kids loved their huge fruit cookies and their chocolate and white cupcakes filled with rich white cream and topped with confectioners' sugar. Their hermits and molasses cookies were also a hit. We couldn't get the original Freihofer's recipe, but the kids agree that these come pretty darned close.

Cookie-Jar Molasses Cookies

about 4 dozen cookies

1¼ cups sugar
1 cup vegetable shortening
1 cup cold black coffee
1 cup molasses
2 eggs

½ teaspoon ground cloves
4 cups all-purpose flour
1 teaspoon baking soda
½ teaspoon salt

Preheat the oven to 350°F. In a large bowl, with an electric beater on medium speed, combine the sugar and shortening until well mixed. Add the coffee, molasses, eggs, and cloves and beat on low speed until thoroughly mixed. Gradually add the flour, baking soda, and salt and continue beating until combined. Drop the dough by heaping tablespoonfuls about 2 inches apart onto ungreased baking sheets. Bake for 10 to 12 minutes, until the edges are browned. Remove to a wire rack to cool completely.

NOTE: When the cookies are cool, sprinkle the tops with a bit of confectioners' sugar, if you'd like.

Freihofer's is a registered trademark of The Charles Freihofer Baking Company, Inc. Photograph courtesy of Robert W. Smith, Troy, N.Y.

SHOWTIME

Goodbye, 1960s! My janitorial supplies company was floundering, our kids were taking music lessons, Chuck needed braces, Steve was approaching his 13th birthday, which meant a bar mitzvah celebration, and everything was getting more and more costly. Out of necessity, a new family business was born.

When we decided to make and decorate everything ourselves for Steve's bar mitzvah in 1969, little did we know what we were getting ourselves into. My sister, Flo, insisted on paying for and making all the food for the Saturday morning luncheon to follow the services at our temple. Thank goodness for Flo. What a spread! I think she expected an army! That's okay. We still laugh about it, and she still makes a mean batch of chopped herring.

We continued the celebration that evening with 300 of our closest friends and relatives. Oh, the planning that went into that party! We transformed the lobby and auditorium of the new community center. The music was lively, the flowers were fragrant, but it was the food that stole the show.

For the entire week leading up to that party, we chopped and rolled, baked and fried in that community center kitchen. And we brought in Marilyn, Judy, and as many of our other friends and relatives as we could round up to help us make hors d'oeuvres, roll meatballs, set tables, and do everything that had to be done. Ethel's salmon mousse, chopped liver, and pickled mushrooms and my hand-sliced corned beef and sweet-and-sour tongue were big hits. Oh, yes, there was my colorful, bountiful fresh fruit centerpiece that I'd built piece by piece to cover an entire table for the cocktail party. It was a real knockout!

The food kept flowing. Our waitresses were great! And when I rolled out a huge block of halvah (a Turkish candy that you must

acquire a taste for) after dessert, we knew something magical had taken place.

After all that hard work and planning (and cleaning up into the wee hours of the night, as well as the entire next day), we had had a successful weekend. We were flooded with phone calls from people who wanted us to cater parties for them. We were physically and mentally exhausted, but we were proud of what we'd all accomplished. On the day of Steve's bar mitzvah, our family was twice blessed. Our son had become a man, and we had become caterers. Amen! (And hold on!)

Salmon Mousse

10 to 15 appetizer-sized servings

1 cup water
1 envelope (0.25 ounce) unflavored gelatin
¼ cup sugar
3 tablespoons white vinegar
2 tablespoons lemon juice
2 teaspoons finely chopped onion
2 teaspoons red or white prepared horseradish

½ teaspoon salt
1 can (16 ounces) red salmon, drained, boned, and flaked
½ cup mayonnaise
¼ cup finely chopped black olives
1 large celery stalk, finely chopped

In a medium-sized saucepan, combine the water and gelatin; let sit for 5 minutes to soften, then heat over low heat until the gelatin dissolves. Add the sugar, vinegar, lemon juice, onion, horseradish, and salt; mix well. Remove from the heat and allow to cool slightly. In a medium-sized bowl, combine the salmon, mayonnaise, olives, and celery. Add the gelatin mixture; mix well. Pour into a 4-cup gelatin mold and chill for several hours, until set. When ready to serve, dip the mold in hot water, just covering the sides of the mold, for 10 seconds, then quickly invert onto a serving plate that is larger than the mold. Gently shake the mold to loosen it. Slice and serve.

139

None of us will ever forget our very first paid catering job. It was simply (hah!) a delivery of platters of finger sandwiches. Well, the kids helped, and Ethel and I stayed up all night decorating these tiny open-faced tuna, salmon, and egg salad sandwiches. We diced bell peppers, sliced pimientos and green and black olives for making a different design on each sandwich, and chopped up parsley and hard-boiled eggs for sprinkling over the tops, along with paprika, alternating colors as we went. We even made radish rosebuds to decorate the doily-lined platters. Boy, did we sweat over that one. And, boy, did we think we were hot stuff after we got paid our big $25! Oh, well, it covered our food expenses. The labor was another story.

Egg Salad Canapés

about 3 dozen canapés

8 hard-boiled eggs, finely chopped
½ cup mayonnaise
¼ teaspoon salt
¼ teaspoon white pepper
8 slices seeded rye bread
1 medium-sized red bell pepper
1 medium-sized green bell pepper
¼ cup pimiento-stuffed whole green olives
¼ cup pitted black olives
3 tablespoons chopped fresh parsley
⅛ teaspoon paprika

In a medium-sized bowl, combine the eggs, mayonnaise, salt, and pepper; mix well. Spread ¼ cup of the egg mixture evenly over each slice of bread, spreading it to the edges. Cut off the crusts, then cut each slice of bread into different bite-sized shapes, such as rectangles, squares, or triangles. If desired, cut out circles using a small cookie cutter or a drinking glass. Cut the bell peppers into strips and/or a variety of shapes. Dice the olives and/or slice them into circles and half-circles. Garnish the top of each canapé with peppers and olives, then sprinkle some with parsley and some with paprika.

Tuna Salad Canapés

about 3 dozen canapés

1 large can (12 ounces)
  water-packed tuna,
  drained and flaked
⅔ cup mayonnaise
6 slices rye bread
1 medium-sized red bell pepper

1 medium-sized green bell pepper
¼ cup pimiento-stuffed whole
  green olives
3 tablespoons chopped
  fresh parsley
⅛ teaspoon paprika

In a medium-sized bowl, combine the tuna and mayonnaise; mix well. Spread ¼ cup of the mixture evenly over each slice of bread, spreading it to the edges. Cut off the crusts, then cut each slice of bread into different bite-sized shapes, such as rectangles, squares, or triangles. If desired, cut out circles using a small cookie cutter or a drinking glass. Cut the bell peppers into strips and/or a variety of shapes. Dice the olives and/or slice them into circles and half-circles. Garnish the top of each canapé with peppers and olives, then sprinkle some with parsley and some with paprika.

NOTE: Be imaginative and make each one different. How you top them is totally up to you.

Every day, every moment is an adventure when you're in the catering business. The weather is a constant concern because it's usually either too hot or too cold for storing and transporting your precious food. Take Ethel's beautiful gelatin molds, for instance.

Ethel has always been our expert wrapper and packer, to this day making sure any food she wraps arrives at its destination intact and without a mess. (You'd think she had stock in plastic wrap!) Of course, she should have helped our friend Judy Paul pack the fricassee when Judy helped us out one fateful day. Delivering a huge pot of it to us the day before a party, Judy stopped her car short and, well, we forgot about serving that fricassee as we cleaned it out of the entire back of Judy's car! After that, none of our food went anywhere unless it was, as Ethel puts it, "wrapped to travel."

To get back to the gelatin molds, Ethel made them with different gelatin flavors and combinations of canned fruit, sour cream, and whipped topping, in a variety of shapes and sizes. She developed an art of getting them out of their molds and onto serving platters in one piece, and still solid. And how'd she make them so light? Try this one and find out. Oh, be sure to treat it gently while transporting it to your next potluck supper!

Citrus Gelatin Mold

12 to 14 servings

1 package (4-serving size)
   lemon-flavored gelatin
1 package (4-serving size)
   orange-flavored gelatin
½ cup sugar
2 cups boiling water

1 cup orange juice
1 container (16 ounces) frozen
   whipped topping, thawed
1 can (17 ounces) fruit cocktail,
   drained

Place the gelatins and sugar in a large bowl; add the boiling water and stir until the gelatins and sugar are completely dissolved. Stir in the orange juice, then cover and chill for about 1 hour, until slightly thickened. Stir in the whipped topping, mixing well. Fold in the drained fruit cocktail until thoroughly combined. Pour into a 10-inch Bundt pan and chill for 4 to 6 hours, or until firm. When ready to serve, dip the mold in warm water, just covering the sides of the mold, for a few seconds, then quickly invert onto a serving plate that is larger than the mold. Gently shake the mold to loosen it. Slice and serve.

J ust as some people judge a book by its cover and a well-dressed man by the shine of his shoes, some people judge a caterer by his or her noodle pudding. Is it too chewy? Does it have enough cinnamon? Does it hold together or fall apart too easily?

The traditional name for it is *kugel*, and it's always been a holiday staple in our family. So, we just took Flo's recipe and multiplied it . . . by a lot! Even though everyone likes it his own way, some with cottage cheese and some without, some with apples and some with pineapple, ours was always a big seller. Sure, every so often we experimented with a new variation, but we always came back to Flo's recipe. And it's *still* the one we all prefer.

Noodle Pudding

9 to 12 servings

1 package (16 ounces) medium egg noodles

6 eggs

1 container (16 ounces) sour cream

1 cup cottage cheese

1 cup sugar

2 teaspoons ground cinnamon

1 teaspoon vanilla extract

¾ teaspoon salt

1½ cups chunky applesauce

½ cup raisins

Preheat the oven to 350°F. Prepare the noodles according to the package directions; drain, rinse, and drain again. In a large bowl, with an electric beater on medium speed, beat the eggs, sour cream, cottage cheese, sugar, cinnamon, vanilla, and salt until well combined. With a spoon, stir in the applesauce, raisins, and noodles. Pour into a 9" × 13" baking dish that has been coated with nonstick vegetable spray. Bake for 60 to 65 minutes, or until the center is set and the sides and top are lightly browned.

As in any good business, we stayed true to the things that had made us successful, but we also kept a close eye on the trends. During the '70s, the desire for international foods grew. Italian and Greek foods became more popular than ever, and even French food, which had long been considered too difficult for the average cook to attempt, came into vogue.

Suddenly, quiche was on menus everywhere. We played around with it and decided it'd be a versatile offering for us, since it could be served as an hors d'oeuvre, appetizer, luncheon dish, or dinner accompaniment. And, made with 2 types of cheeses, heavy cream, eggs, and our secret ingredient, nutmeg, our quiche was second to none, if I do say so myself. For the fillings, we let our imaginations go. Spinach was the most popular, but we also got lots of requests for mixed vegetables, and even smoked salmon. Any way we filled it, our quiche was still a breeze to throw together. And, yes, real men *did* eat our quiche!

Spinach Quiche

6 to 8 servings

1½ cups (6 ounces) shredded
  Cheddar cheese
1½ cups (6 ounces) shredded Swiss
  cheese
1 package (10 ounces) frozen
  chopped spinach, thawed and
  squeezed dry

3 eggs, beaten
1 cup heavy cream
1 teaspoon onion powder
¼ teaspoon black pepper
¼ teaspoon ground nutmeg
One 9-inch unbaked pie shell

Preheat the oven to 350°F. In a medium-sized bowl, combine all the ingredients except the pie crust; mix until thoroughly combined. Pour into the pie shell and bake for 45 to 50 minutes, or until firm in the center. Remove from the oven and let cool for 5 minutes before cutting.

Call us crazy, call us old-fashioned, just call us. And call us they did! Weddings, bar mitzvahs, graduations, cocktail parties, and corporate events were being booked at a phenomenal rate. Ginsburg Caterers was thriving, to the point where I began to phase out my failing janitorial supplies business completely.

We believed—and still do—that our catering success was due to a few things: One—Even as our business got very large, Ethel and I (and usually the kids, too) were at every party we did. We were firm in our belief that she had to be in the kitchen and I had to be in the party room to keep everything running smoothly, so every party received our personal touch. Two—We never ran out of food. Remember what I told you earlier about my dad's philosophy rubbing off on me? Well, it made all the difference when we were catering, since people who hired us were confident that their guests would be able to have as much food as they wanted. And three—We made everything from scratch ourselves, except the breads and desserts. No premade hors d'oeuvres, sauces, or even salad dressings (my particular pride and joy) would find their way onto our tables. Uh-uh! We served homemade food made with fresh ingredients. That way, we ensured that every taste was exclusively ours. That philosophy obviously worked, because we flourished in that business for 18 years before Mr. Food took off and drastically changed our lives yet again.

Creamy Pepper Dressing

about 3 cups

2 cups mayonnaise
¾ cup milk
2 tablespoons grated Parmesan
    cheese
1 tablespoon cider vinegar

1 tablespoon black pepper
1 teaspoon finely chopped onion
1 teaspoon garlic salt
Dash of hot pepper sauce
Dash of Worcestershire sauce

Combine all the ingredients in a medium-sized bowl; whisk until well mixed. Cover and chill for at least 1 hour before serving.

NOTE: In addition to being a dynamite dressing for tossed salads, this also makes a great dip for fresh-cut veggies.

If you think catering a party was difficult, you should have seen the hosts at our first meeting with them, drooling over their food choices and trying to decide what to have. Often they left the smaller decisions up to us, such as which hors d'oeuvres to serve. Chinese chicken, rumaki (ours was chicken livers wrapped in corned beef), Cantonese knishes, pigs in a blanket, potato pancakes, and our other handmade hot hors d'oeuvres were always in great demand.

For years, people tried to get our recipes out of us, and now, finally, we're sharing our secrets.

Pigs in a Blanket

about 6 dozen pieces

½ cup all-purpose flour
1 egg, beaten
⅛ teaspoon salt
⅓ cup regular (not light) beer

3 cups vegetable oil
6 hot dogs (about 1 pound), cut
    into ½-inch pieces

In a medium-sized bowl, combine the flour, egg, and salt; mix well. Gradually stir in the beer. In a large saucepan, heat the oil over medium heat until very hot but not smoking. In batches, dip the hot dog pieces into the batter, coating completely, and carefully place in the hot oil. Cook about a dozen pieces at a time for 2 minutes, or until golden; reduce the heat if necessary to keep the hot dogs from burning. Remove from the oil with a slotted spoon and drain on paper towels. Serve immediately, or keep warm in a low oven until ready to serve.

Potato Pancakes

8 to 10 pancakes

4 medium-sized baking potatoes (about 1½ pounds), peeled and grated
1 small onion, finely chopped
1 egg, beaten

½ cup all-purpose flour
1 teaspoon baking powder
½ teaspoon salt
¼ teaspoon white pepper
⅓ cup vegetable oil

Place the potatoes and onions in a strainer and press down on them with the back of a large spoon to extract excess moisture. If they're still watery, wrap them in a clean dish towel and squeeze to extract the remaining moisture. Place in a large bowl and add the egg; mix well. Gradually add the flour, baking powder, salt, and pepper, mixing well. Heat the oil in a large skillet over medium-high heat. Pour ¼ cup of batter per pancake into the skillet, being careful not to crowd the skillet. Fry the pancakes for 5 to 6 minutes, until golden on both sides, turning halfway through the cooking. (If you like them crisper, fry until they're flecked with brown.) Drain on paper towels and serve warm.

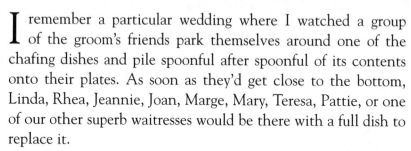

I remember a particular wedding where I watched a group of the groom's friends park themselves around one of the chafing dishes and pile spoonful after spoonful of its contents onto their plates. As soon as they'd get close to the bottom, Linda, Rhea, Jeannie, Joan, Marge, Mary, Teresa, Pattie, or one of our other superb waitresses would be there with a full dish to replace it.

When one of the guys finally came up to ask me what they were eating, he went absolutely white. He couldn't believe he'd been eating tongue. Yes, cow's tongue. I watched him tell the group, and most of them shrugged and dug in for more. Beef tongue was a regular at our house, since my dad had always done his own butchering. In fact, the recipe for the sweet-and-sour tongue they'd been eating was a contest winner for me long before I became a caterer. A local newspaper had held a recipe contest, and I won!

Later in our catering days, we'd sometimes substitute miniature hot dogs for tongue, since some people were squeamish about the idea of serving tongue. I guess they hadn't grown up with it as a regular habit in their homes. Anyway, I'll never forget the look on that guy's face. . . .

Sweet-and-Sour Hot Dogs

4 to 6 servings

12 gingersnap cookies, crushed
1¾ cups firmly packed light
   brown sugar
1 can (6 ounces) tomato paste
1 cup ketchup
½ cup raisins

¼ cup water
2 teaspoons dry mustard
1 teaspoon lemon juice
½ teaspoon ground ginger
1 pound miniature hot dogs

In a soup pot, combine all the ingredients except the hot dogs over medium heat; mix well. Stir in the hot dogs and cook for 4 to 5 minutes. Reduce the heat to low and simmer for 30 minutes, or until the hot dogs are thoroughly heated, stirring occasionally.

Oh, the hustle and bustle just before the guests arrived! The staff would scurry around placing the chopped liver, salmon mousse, cocktail bread, and other cold hors d'oeuvres on the cocktail tables. I'd be rushing to put the finishing touches on my fruit centerpiece, and then, just minutes before the guests were to walk into a cocktail party, I'd run out to freshen up and change into party clothes. Sometimes I'd change in the bathroom, if one was accessible; other times I'd find an available closet, or even use the back of our truck or van. Then I'd wash my hands, grab a serving fork, choose the most tender corned beef on the stove, and off I'd go with it to my carving cart. There I'd stand for the next half-hour or so (we didn't want cocktail parties to go on too long, spoiling the guests' dinner appetites), visiting with the guests, of course, while carving ever-so-thin slices of corned beef to pile onto miniature dinner knots (rolls) that I'd cut open just enough on one side so that the meat wouldn't fall out the other side.

We knew what a treat our corned beef was by the number of guests lined up in front of me at every party for seconds and thirds!

Glazed Corned Beef

6 to 8 servings

One 2½- to 3-pound cooked corned beef brisket *or* raw corned beef brisket, cooked according to the package directions

½ cup apricot preserves
1 tablespoon honey
1 tablespoon prepared yellow mustard

Preheat the oven to 400°F. Line a 9" × 13" baking pan with aluminum foil and fill with 1 inch of water; place the corned beef in the pan and cover tightly with foil. Bake for 1½ hours, or until very tender, adding additional water as needed. Remove from the oven and drain off the liquid. In a small bowl, combine the remaining ingredients and brush over the corned beef. Roast for 30 minutes, uncovered, until the glaze caramelizes. Slice across the grain into thin slices.

In the midst of all those parties, each one being a well-rehearsed performance of its own, I became involved in community theatre, with a little nudging from my cousin Sally. I had been interested in theatre in high school, but there hadn't been a lot of time for it before—not that there was now. I just fell into a few special roles and I loved how acting took me to a new place, a place where I could leave my work and home responsibilities behind for a few hours at a time, and take on a whole different personality.

One of my first shows was *Tevye and His Daughters*, a beautiful play on which the musical *Fiddler on the Roof* was based. In that play, Tevye had seven daughters, so I brought Caryl along to play the youngest daughter, who appeared in all of two scenes. Another big show for me was Woody Allen's *Don't Drink the Water*. It was a hilarious show that was a hit for Albany Civic Theatre. I'm the good-looking one with the funny hat and cigar. After that show, I was invited to audition for a production of *Fiddler on the Roof* that was being done in our area. The lead character, again, was Tevye the dairyman. Tevye immediately reminded me of my father, and by the time the show ran, Tevye was a part of me. We were so much alike, Tevye and I, each practicing our beliefs, protecting our families, and, most of all, following the beautiful traditions of our ancestors.

Caryl played one of Tevye's daughters this time, too, and Ethel helped out backstage. *Fiddler on the Roof* has always held special meaning for our family. I was very lucky to discover Tevye.

Some people from a local supermarket chain happened to catch my *Fiddler* performance, and they offered me a television commercial. Right after I did the Sweet Life brand commercial, again as Tevye, our friend Mimi Scott asked me to appear on her local morning magazine-style TV talk show. I appeared as myself, making an easy recipe. Mimi got so much mail after my appearance that she asked me to be a weekly regular. I figured, "Why not?" But before my next appearance, we discussed how she should introduce me. You see, after my first appearance, when Mimi had used my real name and said that I was a local caterer, Ethel and I had received a phone call in the middle of the night from someone asking us to cater her daughter's wedding. I wasn't fond of middle-of-the-night phone calls, so I told Mimi to introduce me the next time as Mr. Caterer, Mr. Pan, Mr. Food, anything but Art Ginsburg. Well, she did it. She introduced me as Mr. Food, and the name stuck! Soon after that, I thought about the song in the musical *Gypsy* called "You've Gotta Get a Gimmick," and decided I needed a special way to end each of my segments. So, at the end of my next segment, I just came out with, "Ooh it's so good!!" and that stuck, too. It just seemed to work every time. And when people came up to me at the supermarket and asked if I was the "Ooh it's so good!!" man, I knew I had found my something special.

As fortunate as I was to find Tevye, I was fortunate again to find Mr. Food. Every week, when our family gathered together to welcome the sabbath and enjoy Ethel's roasted chicken, we expressed our thanks for all our blessings, just as Tevye and his family had through the touching song "Sabbath Prayer," in *Fiddler*. Ethel, Steve, Caryl, Chuck, and I knew we had a great deal to be thankful for—and we still do.

Friday-Night Roasted Chicken

3 to 4 servings

1 tablespoon vegetable oil
1 teaspoon paprika
1 teaspoon onion powder
1 teaspoon garlic powder

1 teaspoon salt
½ teaspoon black pepper
One 2½- to 3-pound chicken

Preheat the oven to 350°F. In a small bowl, combine all the ingredients except the chicken. Place the chicken in a roasting pan and rub the seasoning mixture over the chicken until completely coated. Bake, uncovered, for 1½ hours, or until the chicken skin is crispy and the juices run clear, using a pastry brush to baste occasionally with the pan juices.

"FIDDLER ON THE ROOF" STARRING ROLES---Barbara Benezet of Newtonville, a junior at Shaker High School Arthur Ginsburg of Troy, playing Tevye, the male lead a senior at Troy High School Toni Levitto of Latham a Siena Sharon Miller of Troy, a senior at Troy High School Toni Levitto of Latham a Siena freshman, pictured above left to right, are 3 girls playing the marriageable daughters of Tevye, the milkman in "Fiddler on the Roof" being presented this w on Thursday, Friday and Saturday, (Nov. 18, 19 and 20) at 8:15 p.m. in Shaker School. This is the 12th musical production to be given by the Triune Musical pany, Inc.

Catering and acting left little time for anything else. We spent the weekdays planning, ordering, and cooking for parties, we spent a good deal of our weeknights meeting with prospective clients at our home (when I didn't have show rehearsals), and on the weekends, we did parties. We were surrounded by wonderful food, but sometimes we just needed a change. That's where Villa Valenti came in!

It was a tiny family-run Italian restaurant on the outskirts of Troy. The food was all made from scratch and served by Emma and Sam Valenti and their kids. They loved hosting us because we enjoyed their food so heartily. And we loved everything the Valentis made! When Emma saw us coming, she'd light the extra ovens, 'cause while we were enjoying our mounds of antipasto and crusty Italian bread, she'd whip up some of everything she had, from smooth manicotti to feathery-light meatballs, tender-as-can-be veal Parmigiana, and veal Marsala. The Valentis' food and friendship kept us coming back. Today, that friendship is stronger than ever, and the food as delicious as ever. I guess the love that goes into it makes all the difference.

In later years, we topped off our meals with desserts made by the Valenti daughters—chocolate ice cream cake roll (Steve's absolute favorite) and spumoni. We've loved their food for so long that, together, we've come up with an inimitable pasta sauce that they make under the Mr. Food name. It's another way we keep our family traditions going strong.

Villa Valenti's Eggplant Rollatini

4 to 6 servings

4 eggs, beaten
1 teaspoon salt, divided
1 teaspoon black pepper, divided
2 cups seasoned bread crumbs
About ½ cup olive oil
2 medium-sized eggplants, peeled
and cut lengthwise into
⅛-inch-thick slices
(about 16 slices total)

1 jar (26 to 30 ounces) spaghetti
sauce, divided
2 containers (15 ounces each)
ricotta cheese
2 cups (8 ounces) shredded
mozzarella cheese, divided
¼ cup grated Parmesan cheese
1 teaspoon garlic powder

Preheat the oven to 350°F. Place the eggs, ½ teaspoon salt, and ½ teaspoon pepper in a shallow dish; mix well. Place the bread crumbs in another shallow dish. Heat 2 tablespoons oil in a large skillet over medium-high heat. Dip the eggplant slices into the eggs, then into the bread crumbs, coating evenly. Sauté, a few slices at a time, for 3 to 4 minutes, until golden, turning halfway through the cooking and adding more oil as necessary. Place the fried eggplant on a paper-towel–lined platter. Reserve 1 cup of the spaghetti sauce and pour the remaining sauce over the bottom of a 9" × 13" baking dish. In a large bowl, combine the ricotta cheese, 1 cup mozzarella cheese, the Parmesan cheese, garlic powder, and the remaining ½ teaspoon each salt and pepper; mix well. Place the fried eggplant on a work surface and spread ¼ cup of the ricotta cheese mixture over the top of each. Roll up jelly-roll fashion and place seam side down in the baking dish. Pour the reserved 1 cup spaghetti sauce over the eggplant rolls and top with the remaining 1 cup mozzarella cheese. Bake for 35 to 40 minutes, or until the sauce is hot and bubbly and the cheese has melted.

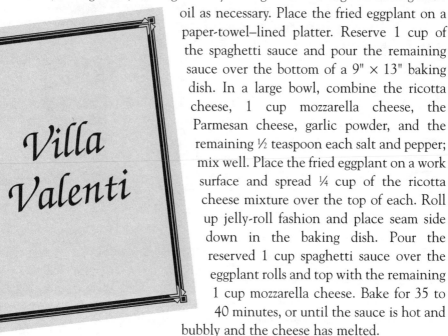

Villa
Valenti

Emma's Veal Marsala

4 servings

¼ cup all-purpose flour
1 teaspoon salt
½ teaspoon black pepper
1 pound veal cutlets
2 tablespoons olive oil
2 garlic cloves, minced

1 jar (6 ounces) sliced mushrooms,
    drained
2 tablespoons butter
2 tablespoons chopped fresh
    parsley
1 cup Marsala wine

In a shallow dish, combine the flour, salt, and pepper. Coat the veal in the flour mixture. In a large nonstick skillet, heat the oil over medium-high heat and sauté the garlic and the veal pieces for 4 to 5 minutes, until the veal is browned, turning halfway through the cooking. Remove the veal to a platter; set aside. Add the mushrooms, butter, and parsley to the skillet and stir until the butter melts. Stir in the wine, then return the veal to the skillet and cook for 2 to 4 minutes, until the sauce thickens and the veal is warmed through, turning halfway through the cooking. Serve immediately.

The catering was going stronger than ever, so every so often we'd get bold and offer a new dish or two to keep our parties different and exciting. Often we'd go back to classic family recipes and adapt them to meet our catering standards—like we

Once in a while, after servi dinner, we'd take a quick sp on the dance floor!

did with stuffed cabbage. We took the assembly-line approach to making them. The auto makers could have learned a thing or two from us! Making hundreds of these at a time was a real family affair. Mmm, I can still remember that rich aroma when they simmered in the oven in their flavorful sauce.

Stuffed Cabbage

8 to 12 servings

1 large cabbage, cored
2 cups firmly packed light brown sugar
20 gingersnap cookies, crushed
1 can (28 ounces) crushed tomatoes, undrained
1 can (6 ounces) tomato paste
1 cup raisins

1 medium-sized onion, chopped, divided
½ cup lemon juice
1 pound ground beef
1 cup cooked rice
1 egg
2 teaspoons salt
½ teaspoon black pepper

Preheat the oven to 350°F. Place the cabbage cored side down in 1 inch of water in a large saucepan; cover and steam over low heat for 30 to 40 minutes, or until fork-tender. Drain and set aside. In a large bowl, combine the sugar, gingersnaps, tomatoes and their juice, the tomato paste, raisins, ½ cup of the chopped onion, and the lemon juice. In another large bowl, combine the ground beef, rice, egg, the remaining onion, the salt, and pepper. Place 2 cups of the tomato mixture in the bottom of a 9"× 13" baking dish that has been coated with nonstick vegetable spray. Peel a cabbage leaf off the head and cut off the thick stem end. Then place ¼ cup of the meat mixture in the center of the leaf. Using your hands and starting at the core end, make a roll about 1" × 2½", folding over the sides and rolling loosely. Place the roll seam side down in the tomato mixture in the baking dish. Repeat with the remaining cabbage leaves and meat mixture. Spoon the remaining tomato mixture evenly over the tops of the rolls. Tent tightly with aluminum foil. Bake for 1½ hours, or until the beef is no longer pink and the cabbage is very tender. Serve immediately.

"Looking for a change-of-pace side dish to serve with your entrée?" Ethel and I would have *just* the suggestion to match every host's menu to his or her personality. Unless we had to check out a new party location, we'd meet with clients at our home to discuss everything from the costs and the party time to the colors, table settings, and, of course, the menu. What would go best with the stuffed capon breast at a fall luncheon—potato crepes? Maybe the potato pudding squares would do the trick. . . .

Potato Pudding Squares

6 to 9 servings

5 large all-purpose potatoes
    (about 2 pounds), cut into
    large chunks
1 medium-sized onion,
    cut into large chunks
2 eggs

⅔ cup vegetable oil
1½ teaspoons salt
½ teaspoon white pepper
½ cup all-purpose flour
1 tablespoon chopped fresh parsley

Preheat the oven to 350°F. In a food processor, combine the potatoes, onion, eggs, oil, salt, and pepper. Process until the vegetables are coarsely chopped and place in a large bowl; stir in the flour and parsley. Pour into a 7" × 11" baking dish that has been coated with nonstick vegetable spray. Bake for 1 hour and 20 minutes, or until the top is golden brown. Let cool slightly and cut into squares.

NOTE: This works best if allowed to cool for about 20 minutes before cutting. It's also a great dish to make ahead of time and reheat.

Mention Ginsburg Caterers and people not only thought of our delicious food and beautiful fruit displays, they thought of our excellent service, too. We know we were lucky to have a truly devoted staff working both on the party floor and in the kitchen. Under Ethel's direction, Maddy, Lori, Paul, and Eleanor always kept our kitchen clean and organized. The party floor was my domain, and our waitresses, busboys, and bartenders were a pleasure to work with. They were hard-working homemakers, office workers, salesmen, and students—with a few food service professionals in the mix, too. Even Michael Cocca, Teresa Arakelian (now Pepe), and Frank Cooper, and others of our kids' buddies, devoted countless hours over the years to working alongside us all.

We cultivated good relationships with our help—and many of those relationships are still thriving today. They knew that we respected them and how hard they worked, and, in return, we were rewarded with their outstanding work and attention to detail. They took as much pride in their work as we did; we all worked together as family and friends.

When we catered sit-down dinners, we had a unique way of serving the main course. I would lead the serving team. As we booked bigger and bigger parties, requiring more teams, Steve and Chuck donned tuxedos and were promoted to team leaders; then we enlisted our friends Alan Roer and Stan Ruderman as maître d'/team leaders, too. The leader would wheel his cart from table to table as his team brought out hot platters of food for each one. He would flambé the sesame chicken, or garnish the roast prime eye of the rib or other entrée, before serving it along with a steaming-hot potato crepe or other side dish to each person. At the same time, the team would place an assortment of vegetables and condiments on that table for family-style serving. I often dimmed the lights to enhance the tableside "show." After all, we eat with our eyes as well as our mouths!

Sesame Chicken

6 servings

6 boneless, skinless chicken breast halves (1½ to 2 pounds total)	2 teaspoons dried thyme
½ cup all-purpose flour	1 teaspoon ground caraway
2 eggs, beaten	1 teaspoon garlic powder
1 cup seasoned bread crumbs	1½ teaspoons salt
⅓ cup sesame seeds	¼ teaspoon black pepper
	½ cup vegetable oil

Preheat the oven to 350°F. With a meat mallet, pound the chicken to about a ½-inch thickness; set aside. Place the flour in a shallow dish and the eggs in another shallow dish; in a third shallow dish, combine the bread crumbs, sesame seeds, thyme, caraway, garlic powder, salt, and pepper; mix well. Dip the chicken into the flour, then the eggs, then the bread crumb mixture, coating evenly with each. In a large skillet, heat the oil over medium heat. Sauté the chicken in the hot oil for 4 minutes, until golden on both sides, turning halfway through the cooking. Remove the chicken to a large rimmed baking sheet that has been coated with nonstick vegetable spray. Bake the chicken for 10 to 12 minutes, or until no pink remains and the juices run clear.

Potato Crepes

12 crepes

1 can (14½ ounces) ready-to-use
  chicken broth
2 eggs
1 cup all-purpose flour
¼ teaspoon salt
6 cups warm mashed potatoes

1 tablespoon dried parsley flakes
½ teaspoon onion powder
½ teaspoon garlic powder
½ teaspoon white pepper
About ¼ cup vegetable oil

Preheat the oven to 325°F. In a large bowl, combine the chicken broth
and eggs; mix well. Gradually whisk in the flour and salt until the batter
is smooth. In another large bowl, combine the mashed potatoes, parsley
flakes, onion powder, garlic powder, and pepper; set aside. Brush an
8- to 10-inch skillet with oil and heat over
medium-low heat. Pour ¼ cup of the
batter into the hot skillet, gently tilting
the skillet in a circular motion to distrib-
ute the batter evenly over the bottom.
Cook for about 2 to 3 minutes, or until
the surface appears dry and the bottom is
golden-flecked. Flip the crepe out onto a
piece of waxed paper and cover with
another piece of waxed paper. Repeat with
the remaining batter until you've made 12
crepes, brushing the skillet with oil each
time. Form ½ cup of the mashed potato
mixture into a log in the center of each
crepe. Fold one side over the potato mixture
and roll up crepe-style. Place the crepes seam
side down on a baking sheet that has been
coated with nonstick vegetable spray. Brush
the tops of the crepes with vegetable oil and
bake for 25 to 30 minutes, or until the crepes
are golden and heated through.

When it came to deciding on what type of music to have for a party or event, we always told our clients, "The music makes the party." After all, if the music wasn't right, then no matter how wonderful the food, the party would be lacking something.

And at each party, there were guests who wanted to hear different kinds of music, whether it was the cha-cha, swing, or rock 'n' roll. They'd make requests of the band; some were easy to satisfy, others weren't. It was the same with us.

Even though we'd worked with the hosts to choose just the right foods, there was usually an odd request or two from guests who wanted something other than what they were being served. As with the band, some requests were easy to satisfy on short notice, others weren't!

If the hosts knew in advance that some of their guests were vegetarians, they'd be sure to let us know ahead of time. But most of the time we were ready for that simple a request anyway. I had taken to making fresh vegetable pancakes to have on hand for every party. (Our staff and kids would eat them if no one asked for

them!) The pancakes were so good that sometimes we got requests for them from nonvegetarians. And most of the time they'd be very happy with them . . . that is, until they saw the juicy prime rib being served to the rest of their table!

Vegetable Pancakes

about 4 dozen pancakes

3 cups shredded zucchini,
    squeezed dry
1 cup shredded carrots,
    squeezed dry
8 eggs
½ cup grated Parmesan cheese
⅔ cup all-purpose flour
¼ cup chopped onion

½ cup plus 2 teaspoons olive or
    vegetable oil, divided, plus
    extra if needed
1 teaspoon baking powder
2 teaspoons salt
1 teaspoon black pepper
⅓ cup plain dry bread crumbs

In a large bowl, combine the zucchini, carrots, eggs, Parmesan cheese, flour, onion, 2 teaspoons oil, the baking powder, salt, and pepper; mix well. Stir in the bread crumbs. Heat ¼ cup oil in a large skillet over medium heat. Carefully drop the batter by heaping tablespoonfuls into the hot oil and cook for about 4 minutes, until golden on both sides, turning halfway through the cooking. Remove to a covered platter to keep warm. Continue cooking until no batter remains, adding additional oil as needed.

NOTE: Try topping these with a little salsa for a great side dish or main course. You can even make them a little smaller and serve as an appetizer.

Our family often ate the "by-products" from our parties . . . like leftover fruit turned into fruit salad or cooked vegetables turned into soup. What I loved most were the short ribs and rib bones from the prime ribs, which we'd make barbecue-style.

First we'd slow-roast the ribs in a bit of water, just until tender. Then we'd slather on our homemade barbecue sauce and finish them off either in the oven or on the grill, weather permitting, naturally. There never seemed to be a shortage of ribs at our house. Thank goodness, 'cause we always knew we had a meal nearby if we served them up with a crisp salad, some crusty bread, and a load of napkins.

Sweet-and-Sour Short Ribs

4 to 6 servings

4 pounds beef short ribs
½ teaspoon salt
¼ teaspoon black pepper
½ cup ketchup
⅓ cup firmly packed light
   brown sugar

2 tablespoons white vinegar
1 tablespoon paprika
1 clove garlic, minced
1 teaspoon onion powder

Preheat the oven to 350°F. Place the short ribs in a 9" × 13" baking pan and sprinkle with the salt and pepper. Add ¼ inch of water to the pan. Cover tightly with aluminum foil and bake for 1 hour. Remove from the oven and carefully remove the foil. Carefully pour off most of the liquid from the roasting pan. In a small bowl, combine the remaining ingredients; mix well and generously brush the sauce all over the ribs. Re-cover the meat with the aluminum foil and return to the oven for 1 hour, or until fork-tender.

PLACES I'VE GONE, PEOPLE I'VE MET

In 1976, Steve graduated from the State University of New York at Cobleskill with a degree in food service administration, then joined Ethel and me full-time to help out with the catering and also to help me with the production of my television segments. Chuck was still in high school, not quite ready to think about college. And Caryl went off to the State University of New York at Oswego to pursue her degree in music performance.

I remember going to visit Caryl after she'd had a chance to get settled into college life. She had been telling us she had found this restaurant that we just *had* to try. It turned out to be a breakfast diner called Wade's. You have to be prepared to stand in line outside the place, because it's so tiny. But we found out, as many Upstate New Yorkers had known for years, that Wade's is worth waiting for. Their cook, "Slim," is the quickest egg handler I've ever seen, and his omelets and home fries are out of this world! But we

Their cook, "Slim," is the quickest egg handler I've ever seen. · · · ·

Me with Howard, Caryl, and Chuck—my Oswego contingent!

all agreed that the best part of breakfast at Wade's is the homemade raisin toast. They won't share their secret recipe, so I guess we have to settle for making regular pilgrimages to Oswego to enjoy it. Actually, that was not hard for us for a while, since the year after Caryl graduated, Chuck began his freshman year at Oswego!

Oswego was important to all of us for another reason: It started early in Caryl's freshman year when she called Ethel and me and announced, "Have I got a guy for you!" She had said he was for *us*. What exactly did she mean?

It turned out that she'd met a freshman from Syracuse, New York, through a mutual friend. His name was Howard Rosenthal and he'd been working for a Syracuse caterer for many years and had even begun doing some of his own catering. She wanted us to meet him. Well, as they say, the rest is history!

Howard immediately fit in with the rest of our family, and he began working with us on his available weekends. He left Oswego in his sophomore year to pursue a degree at Cobleskill, as Steve had. He continued to keep in touch with us and work with us on and off for years, even catering Caryl's wedding with us, then doing Steve's wedding on his own, since we were out of the catering business totally by then.

Howard's own Syracuse catering company, Yankel and Company, thrived for over 14 years, but then we made him an offer he and his wife, Patty, couldn't refuse. We asked Howard to join us as we took our entire Mr. Food operation to Fort Lauderdale. It took a lot of planning on all of our parts, but we made it happen, and Patty and Howard are key members of our Mr. Food team today. Thank goodness for Oswego! Caryl was right . . . she *did* have a guy for us!

"Have I got a guy for you . . .

Howard Rosenthal!"

After writing this last chapter, it didn't take me long to realize that I was going to have to do another book like this one . . . because I've easily got another book's worth of memories to share!

My wonderful fans and TV station contacts all around the country have become like an extended family to me. And I wish I could have included twice as many stories and photos in this book. But I've had only enough room to scratch the surface here, so if I haven't mentioned you in these pages, I hope you know that you're in my heart and in my memories, and I'll try to share your stories another time.

So to everyone I've shared a meal, a plane trip, or a chuckle with over the years, I thank you. The best gift you can give is a part of yourself, and you will be forever in my thoughts.

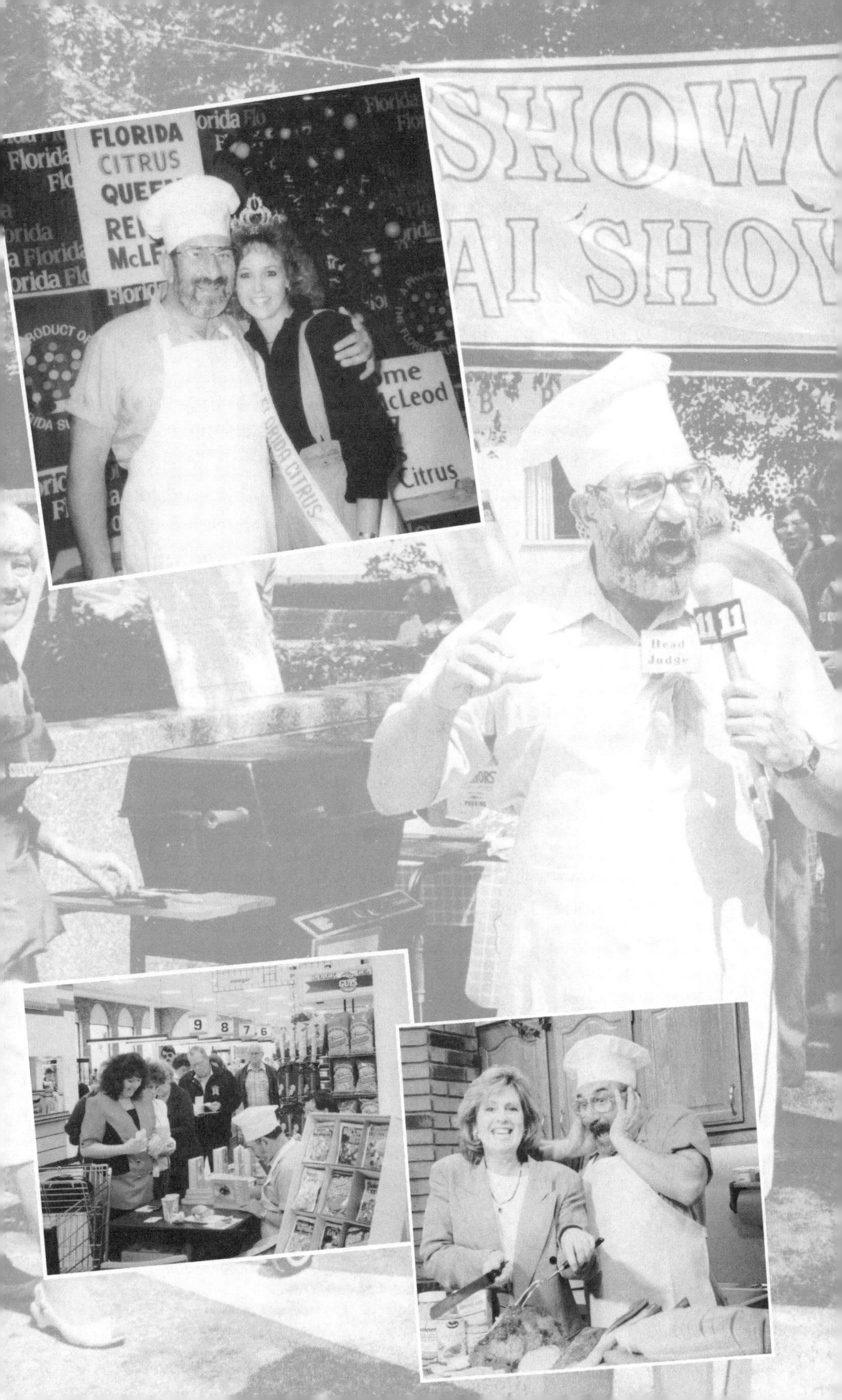
FLORIDA
CITRUS
FLORIDA CITRUS
Citrus
Head
Judge

With the catering business in full swing and the Mr. Food show taking off, time became more and more valuable to us as a family. We were told about a place by the ocean in Rhode Island that was off the beaten path, so we decided to drive the 4 hours from Troy. As we pulled into Narragansett late one July night, we thought we'd made a huge mistake. We didn't see anybody, we couldn't see the beach, and nothing was open!

Fortunately, Narragansett looked much better to us the next day, after we'd had a good night's sleep and done some exploring. In fact, we liked it so much that we've returned there every year since, for a few years with just the kids, then with friends and my mom, and, years later, with our grandchildren. Lots more people have discovered Narragansett over the years, and it's grown incredibly since our first trip there.

Nearby Providence, Rhode Island, was one of my early Mr. Food show cities, too, so I've come to think of Rhode Island as one of my homes away from home. The miles of sandy beaches (where we'd enjoy our homemade tuna sandwiches with Del's frozen lemonade. . . . Mmm!), down-to-earth friends (who are wonderful cooks and bakers, too!), endless availability of fresh seafood (we'd go right to the docks to buy it from the fishermen), and countless wonderful restaurants, like Captain Jack's, the Spain Restaurant, Red Rooster Tavern, and Venus de Milo, have kept me going back. We all love Rhode Island.

Boiled Lobster

2 servings

4 quarts water
¼ cup salt

Two 1½-pound live Maine
lobsters

Place the water and salt in a soup pot. Bring to a boil over high heat. One at a time, grasp the lobsters securely with a pair of kitchen tongs or by cupping your hand around the back of each and plunge each lobster head-first into the boiling water. Cover and return to a boil. Boil for 8 to 9 minutes, or until the lobsters are bright red. Remove the lobsters with tongs and serve immediately. (See Note for serving assistance!)

NOTE: This is how you tackle a whole boiled lobster: Allow the lobster to cool slightly, then twist off the claws and crack each with a lobster cracker or nutcracker. Pull out the meat with a small fork. Remove the tail from the lobster by bending it back until it cracks. Break off the fins at the base of the tail and push the meat out of the shell; cut it into bite-sized chunks. Pull off the skinny lobster legs and suck them as you would a straw, to remove any meat or juices. This is really worth the effort but be careful—the shells can be sharp! And, if you'd like, serve it with melted butter on the side.

After Mimi Scott's *Coffee Break* TV show went off the air in Albany, my regular Mr. Food appearances as part of her program turned into my own segment, which I self-produced at Albany's WAST–TV. The spot continued to grow in popularity and I decided to approach syndicators about distributing it to other stations around the country. Well, no one was interested. They didn't understand the attraction of a down-to-earth guy helping other busy working people make quick and easy food for themselves and their families. Some of the tapes I'd sent out were even returned unopened!

Undaunted, I decided to try syndicating it myself. And WKBW–TV and WTVH–TV, in Buffalo and Syracuse, New York, respectively, decided to give Mr. Food a try! Six other Northeast stations followed! Hallelujah! Then I was introduced to the Kings, and my life changed yet again.

With Mickey Rooney and Michael King . . .

Brothers Roger and Michael King run a family business, too. It's known as King World Productions and currently syndicates *The Oprah Winfrey Show*, *Jeopardy!*, *Wheel of Fortune*, *Inside Edition*, *American Journal*, and *Rolonda*, among many others. I have been fortunate to have King World grow the syndication of the Mr. Food insert to over 130 television markets (that's over 400 U.S. cities!) since the early '80s. And I've also been fortunate to share many meals and good times with Roger and Michael and their families.

So, when we asked these brothers, who live on opposite coasts, to share their favorite foods with us, we were amazed to get the same answer from both: a tuna salad sandwich with lettuce and tomato! Now, that's my kind of lunch!

As for dinner, Paul Cain, Michael King's personal chef, sent me one of Michael's favorite recipes, Spaghetti with Turkey-Garlic Sauce. Ooh, is it yummy!

I also got a chance to meet with Michael St. Angelo, private chef to Roger and Raemali King. He was kind enough to share one of their family's favorite recipes with me and, let me tell you, it's now a favorite with *my* family, too. Chef Michael shared something else with me—he told me that *his* wife uses my cookbooks when she needs a tasty recipe and is pinched for time! Oh, do I love hearing that!

. . . and Roger King

183

One of Michael King's favorite recipes . . .

Spaghetti with Turkey-Garlic Sauce

6 to 8 servings

2 tablespoons olive oil
2 large onions, chopped
6 garlic cloves, chopped
1½ pounds ground turkey
2 cups water
1½ pounds plum tomatoes,
    coarsely chopped
1 can (12 ounces) tomato paste

1 teaspoon dried oregano
½ teaspoon salt
½ teaspoon black pepper
One 16-ounce package linguine
¼ cup grated Parmesan cheese
2 tablespoons chopped fresh
    parsley

In a soup pot, heat the olive oil over medium-high heat; sauté the onions and garlic for 5 to 7 minutes, until the onions are tender. Add the ground turkey and cook for 4 to 5 minutes, until the turkey is browned and no pink remains. Add the water, tomatoes, tomato paste, oregano, salt, and pepper, and stir until well combined. Reduce the heat to low and simmer for 1½ hours, stirring occasionally. Prepare the linguine according to the package directions; drain, rinse, and drain again. Place on a serving platter and top with the sauce, and then the Parmesan cheese and parsley.

A meal fit for a King . . .

"King-Sized" Italian Veal

6 to 8 servings

¼ cup olive oil
1 cup all-purpose flour
½ teaspoon salt, divided
½ teaspoon black pepper, divided
2 pounds boneless veal shoulder,
    cut into 1-inch cubes
8 garlic cloves, finely chopped
2 large green bell peppers,
    cut into strips
2 large red bell peppers, cut into
    strips
1 large red onion, finely chopped
4 ounces fresh mushrooms, cut into
    quarters (about 2 cups)

2 cans (28 ounces each) whole
    tomatoes, undrained,
    cut into quarters
1½ cups Chianti or other dry
    red wine
1 cup coarsely chopped fresh basil
1 cup coarsely chopped fresh
    Italian parsley
1 teaspoon dried thyme
1 teaspoon dried oregano
¼ teaspoon crushed red pepper
1 cup grated Parmesan cheese

In a soup pot, heat the oil over medium-high heat. Meanwhile, in a large bowl, combine the flour, ¼ teaspoon salt, and ¼ teaspoon black pepper; mix well. Add the veal cubes to the mixture and toss to coat completely. Brown the veal and garlic in the oil for 10 to 15 minutes, stirring frequently. Add the remaining ingredients except the Parmesan cheese. Reduce the heat to low and simmer for 1½ hours, stirring occasionally. Serve topped with the Parmesan cheese.

NOTE: The Kings' favorite way to enjoy this dish is family-style over a pound of fresh-cooked fettuccine. Mmm!

I've always enjoyed playing sports—basketball in my childhood, football in my high school years, golf in my newlywed years (and again now), and, in the 1980s, tennis. So, imagine how I felt when WTVH–TV in Syracuse called and asked if I'd like to participate in a major charitable event they were hosting. What'd they want me to do? Play tennis. "Sure," I said. Play tennis with Bjorn Borg and John McEnroe. "You betcha!" I screamed.

I showed up for the event with just a few extra rackets. After all, these guys were hard hitters! And it was like a dream come true to volley with them. They couldn't possibly play a real game with me and a WTVH anchor as their doubles partners. But it didn't matter, 'cause the real winners were the people who got to dig into the buffet I rolled out onto the tennis court during the match (if you can't beat them, feed them!) and, mainly, the recipients of all the dollars we raised that night.

I showed up . . .
with just a few extra rackets.

Our catering business was always slow in January and February, since not too many people wanted to chance booking events during the worst weather months in the Northeast. So we started taking a weeklong trip to Florida every year with our friends Judy and Aaron Paul; we were able to afford it because we stayed at Aaron's parents' place.

After years of doing this, Ethel and I realized we'd like to live in Florida someday. We eventually got to the point in our business and personal life that enabled us to consider spending part of the year in Florida, then, eventually, moving here completely. And when we did, we felt that a whole new world had opened up to us. It was the best thing we ever did. And we've loved being here so much that all three of our children, Ethel's parents and sister, Suzanne, and my sister, Flo, have all migrated here, too. Of course, that meant moving the entire Mr. Food organization from Troy, so in 1994 we took the plunge. Now everything's under one roof—our offices (which are ever-expanding!), our test kitchens, even our production studio.

Do you know what it's like to be in the Land of Fresh Produce? Well, that's what living in Florida feels like to me. I wake up to the aroma of fresh limes growing right outside my window. On my way to work I pass fields full of vine-ripe tomatoes, corn, beans, cucumbers, strawberries . . . I could go on and on.

Many days I can't resist the temptation to stop for some juicy fresh-picked tomatoes that I can bite into as if they were apples. And the avocados. . . . I love to bring them home to make fresh guacamole. Mmm!

Every morning, when Ethel and I wake up, we realize how fortunate we are to live in this paradise called Florida.

Key Lime Pie

6 to 8 servings

¾ cup graham cracker crumbs
5 tablespoons butter, melted
⅓ cup sugar
3 egg yolks

1½ teaspoons grated lime zest
1 can (14 ounces) sweetened
    condensed milk
⅔ cup Key lime juice (see Note)

Preheat the oven to 350°F. In a large bowl, combine the graham cracker crumbs, butter, and sugar; mix well. Coat the bottom of a 9-inch pie plate with nonstick baking spray, then press the graham cracker mixture over the bottom and up the sides of the plate to form a crust; set aside. In a medium-sized bowl, with an electric beater on medium speed, beat the egg yolks and lime zest for 5 minutes, until fluffy. Gradually add the sweetened condensed milk and continue beating for 3 to 4 minutes. Reduce the speed to low and gradually beat in the lime juice just until combined. Pour the filling into the pie crust and bake for 10 minutes, or until firm in the center. Remove from the oven and let cool on a wire rack, then cover and chill for at least 2 hours before serving. This is best served very cold, so freeze for 15 to 20 minutes before serving.

NOTE: Go ahead and top this with whipped cream or whipped topping and garnish with lime slices, if desired. If you can't find fresh Key limes or Key lime juice, it's okay to substitute regular limes, even though it won't be exactly the same.

Fresh Avocado Dip

about 2 cups

3 ripe avocados, peeled and pitted
1 garlic clove, chopped
½ cup hot or medium salsa
2 teaspoons lemon juice
¼ cup chopped fresh cilantro or
    4 teaspoons dried cilantro

½ teaspoon salt
¼ teaspoon black pepper
1 medium-sized tomato, chopped

Place all the ingredients except the tomato in a medium-sized bowl; mash with a potato masher until chunky. Stir gently until well combined. Pour into a 9-inch pie plate or shallow serving bowl and top with the chopped tomato.

Our move to Florida had even more advantages than we could have imagined. Once we realized that it was a short drive to Walt Disney World from Fort Lauderdale, we were on our way!

Now, most of the other Walt Disney World visitors wore shorts and Mickey Mouse T-shirts. But I had on my white hat and apron. Yup, the fabulous Bryan Wittman and the other wonderful Disney people had worked with me to set up taping segments for some of my shows right from the Magic Kingdom and Epcot. I had to keep reminding myself that what I was doing was work, because, boy, did we have fun!

A few years later I even got to make an appearance at Disneyland. While I was there, I got to visit someone who had become a good friend. No, not Goofy. Well, he is a bit goofy, and that's why we love him so much . . . I'm talking about Bryan Wittman, who now works at Disneyland in California. I've really enjoyed my association with him and all the people at Disney. Bryan, I hope you and the gang invite me back soon so I can add some more Disney magic to each and every "OOH IT'S SO GOOD!!"

W hen I talked about Florida a bit earlier, I didn't mention the restaurants. I saved the restaurants for a whole section of their own, because there are so many here that we love.

Some have been here for so long that they've become institutions, like Miami Beach's Joe's Stone Crab Restaurant. Not only is Joe's famous for its succulent stone crabs (as you see in the photo), but all its food is exceptional. There are plates piled high with Joe's coleslaw, conch fritters (Chuck's favorite), and lyonnaise potatoes (Steve's favorite), and Ethel and Caryl's favorite: slices of perfectly tart real Key lime pie.

A short trip up Miami Beach from Joe's is another institution that we like to frequent, the Rascal House. It's a full-service restaurant/deli/bakery, with a big takeout area, too, so don't be surprised if you have to wait in line to get in. Take my word for it—it's worth the wait. Luckily, co-owner Steve Stamler was generous enough to share his recipe for jumbo macaroons with me. I didn't want to ask for their éclair recipe, too, so we worked on it in our test kitchens and came up with one that's pretty close. This version is easy, easy.

I wish I could take you on a complete South Florida restaurant tour, but I've still got so much to tell you about other places I love. . . .

Joe's Lyonnaise Potatoes

4 to 6 servings

6 medium-sized potatoes,
    peeled and quartered
¾ teaspoon salt
¼ teaspoon black pepper

½ cup vegetable oil
1 medium-sized onion,
    coarsely chopped

Fill a medium-sized saucepan three-quarters full with water and bring to a boil over high heat. Add the potatoes and cook for 10 to 15 minutes, or until fork-tender; drain and set aside to cool slightly. Cut the potatoes into ⅛-inch slices and place in a medium-sized bowl; gently stir in the salt and pepper, then set aside. In a large skillet, heat the oil over medium heat and sauté the onions until browned. Add the onions to the potatoes; mix well. Spread the mixture evenly in the skillet and cook for 12 to 14 minutes over medium heat, until the potatoes are browned, turning halfway through the cooking. Serve immediately.

193

Rascal House Macaroons

about 1 dozen cookies

2 packages (14 ounces each)
    shredded coconut
5 egg whites

1½ cups sugar

Preheat the oven to 350°F. Place the coconut in a large bowl; set aside. In a medium-sized saucepan, combine the egg whites and sugar over medium heat. Cook for 2 to 3 minutes, just until the sugar has dissolved and the mixture is bubbly. Remove from the heat and pour over the coconut; mix well. With your hands, squeeze together ½-cupfuls of the mixture to form slightly rounded mounds. Place 1 inch apart on a baking sheet that has been coated with nonstick baking spray and bake for about 25 minutes, until the macaroons begin to color slightly. Turn off the oven and allow the macaroons to sit for about 15 minutes (with the oven door closed), until they turn golden.

NOTE: You can drizzle the macaroons with melted chocolate before serving, if you want. Just melt 1 cup (6 ounces) semisweet chocolate chips in a small saucepan over medium-low heat and drizzle over the tops.

Bakery-Style Éclairs

10 éclairs

1 cup water
½ cup (1 stick) butter, cut into
    quarters
¼ teaspoon salt
1 cup all-purpose flour
4 eggs, at room temperature

1 pint (2 cups) heavy cream
1 package (4-serving size) instant
    vanilla pudding and pie filling
1 cup confectioners' sugar
3 tablespoons unsweetened cocoa
2 tablespoons plus 1 teaspoon milk

Preheat the oven to 400°F. In a medium-sized nonstick saucepan, bring the water, butter, and salt to a boil over medium-high heat. Add the flour all at once and stir quickly with a wooden spoon until the mixture forms a ball. Remove from the heat. Add 1 egg to the mixture and beat hard with the wooden spoon to blend. Add the remaining eggs one at a time, beating well after each addition. Each egg must be completely blended before the next egg is added. As you beat the dough, it will change from looking almost curdled to smooth. When it is smooth, spoon the dough into a large resealable plastic storage bag and, using scissors, snip off one corner of the bag, making a 1-inch-wide cut. Gently squeeze the bag to form 1" × 4" logs of dough about 2 inches apart on an ungreased large rimmed baking sheet. Bake for 40 to 45 minutes, or until golden and puffy. Remove to a wire rack to cool. In a large bowl, with an electric beater on medium speed, beat the cream until stiff peaks form. Fold in the pudding mix and set aside. In a small bowl, stir together the confectioners' sugar, cocoa, and milk until well mixed. Cut the éclair shells in half lengthwise and spoon the pudding mixture evenly into the bottom of each one. Replace the tops of the éclair shells and spread the cocoa mixture over the tops. Serve immediately, or cover and store in the refrigerator until ready to use.

There we were, late in 1988, once again adjusting to major changes in our business and personal lives. The catering business was behind us, and Mr. Food was growing quickly. We had self-published a small cookbook and it had been selling really well, mainly through mail order. We had a commercial kitchen in our basement, where we prepared the food for the TV shows. Upstairs we had converted a couple of bedrooms into offices and hired Mary Ann Oliver as our first full-time staffer. It was an exciting but uncertain time for us. With our little book and the growing syndication of the TV show, more and more people were becoming Mr. Food fans.

Then, a few days before New Year's Eve, I opened a letter that had been sent to me at WRGB–TV, my Schenectady, New York, station. As I read it, I became more and more excited. "Ethel, Steve," I called, "a literary agent wants to talk to me about publishing a cookbook!"

It was the beginning of a whole new era for us. And here we are, 17 books, 20 staffers, and lots of Mr. Food products later, still happy to be part of the team at William Morrow and Company in New York, and grateful for the insight of our book agent Bill Adler, who brought Mr. Food to them.

In each book I continue to thank Bill, and also Al Marchioni and the others at Morrow who saw the potential of my cookbooks and have continued to support my book efforts. And I never forget to acknowledge my viewers and readers, who keep asking for more books filled with humor, lots of tasty, simple recipes, and pages full of
"OOH IT'S SO GOOD!!"
(I hope to continue for a long time!)

Every March, I put on my green hat, scarf, and gloves and hop on the WLS–TV float in Chicago's St. Patrick's Day parade. Oh, I love Chicago. What a city! Yeah, it's cold at that time of year, but the warmth of my brother and sister Chicagoans makes everything toasty for me.

It sure is great to hear the chants of "OOH IT'S SO GOOD!!" from the crowd. Hey, here I am with Joe Ahearn, the General Manager of WLS. You didn't think I'd brave the Windy City's brisk weather without him, did you?

And how could I leave Chicago on St. Patrick's Day without indulging in corned beef and cabbage? Is it ever good! When I get home, I usually make a big platter of the tender meat and flavorful veggies to relive my parade experiences with Ethel. The only thing missing is the wind whipping off Lake Michigan. She doesn't seem to mind.

PHOTOGRAPH COURTESY OF WLS-TV, CHICAGO, ILL.

Corned Beef and Cabbage

4 to 6 servings

One 2½- to 3-pound corned beef
    brisket
One 2- to 3-pound head of
    cabbage, cut into 4 wedges

6 medium-sized potatoes, peeled
6 large carrots, cut into large
    chunks
1 tablespoon salt

Place the corned beef in a soup pot and add just enough water to cover the meat. Cover and cook over medium heat for 2 hours, or until fork-tender. Remove the meat to a platter, leaving the liquid in the pot. Add the remaining ingredients to the pot and place the meat on top. Bring to a boil over medium heat, then cover and reduce the heat to low. Simmer for 25 to 30 minutes, or until the vegetables are fork-tender. Remove the meat and vegetables to a serving platter. Slice the corned beef across the grain into ¼-inch-thick slices and serve with the vegetables.

NOTE: For even more old-fashioned flavor, add the seasoning packet that comes with the meat to the cooking water.

I look for any chance I get to travel to Chicago. Not only do I go for the big parade in March, but I also try to get there for trade shows, book and media tours, and TV station visits, and there's never a question of where I should go to get a great meal. The city is rich in cultural diversity, and it's full of fabulous restaurants.

The first Chicago steak house I ever visited was Gibson's. While I started on their famous garbage salad (yup, that's the real name), they brought out an ice-cold platter of different types of steak and seafood for me to choose from. Then they cooked it up just right. And I couldn't believe the size of their portions! I'll give you a tip: When you make their garbage salad at home, be sure you have plenty of crusty bread on hand for dunking in the tangy dressing.

PHOTOGRAPH COURTESY OF GIBSON'S STEAK HOUSE, CHICAGO, ILL.

Gibson's Garbage Salad

10 to 12 servings

1 head iceberg lettuce,
    washed, dried, and cut into
    bite-sized pieces
1 head romaine lettuce,
    washed, dried, and cut into
    bite-sized pieces
2 medium-sized tomatoes,
    cut into bite-sized pieces
6 slices (1 ounce each) provolone
    cheese, cut into 2" × ¼" strips
6 ounces Genoa salami, cut into
    2" × ¼" strips
1 can (14 ounces) hearts of palm,
    drained and cut into 1-inch
    pieces

1 can (14 ounces) artichoke hearts,
    drained and quartered
1 jar (7 ounces) roasted red
    peppers, drained and
    cut into strips
1 can (5.75 ounces) large pitted
    black olives, drained
1 jar (16 ounces) peperoncini,
    drained
Garlic Herb Vinaigrette

Combine all the ingredients except the dressing in a very large mixing bowl; toss to mix well. Pour the dressing over the top; toss to coat. Serve immediately.

Garlic Herb Vinaigrette

about 2¼ cups

1½ cups olive oil
⅔ cup red wine vinegar
2 garlic cloves, minced
1 tablespoon chopped fresh parsley
1 teaspoon dried basil

1 teaspoon dried thyme
1 teaspoon dried oregano
½ teaspoon dried chives
2 teaspoons salt

In a medium-sized bowl, whisk all the ingredients until well combined. Pour over Gibson's Garbage Salad or a tossed salad, or cover and chill until ready to use.

When it comes to satisfying my urge for Italian food when I'm in Chicago, I can count on any of the Rosebud restaurants. Now, I'm not someone who goes for fancy decor. I don't usually pay too much attention to what a place looks like, as long as it's clean and has good food. But I have to say that the Rosebud on Taylor has it all. It has etched glass and rich detailed woodwork, and the detail in the dining room matches the detail in the kitchen.

I never know what to order—sizzling veal, tender pasta, or farfalle alla vodka (my son-in-law, Roy's, favorite). It's a perfect combination of bow tie pasta and a rich vodka sauce. When I asked for the recipe, I was honored that their team of chefs agreed to let me share it with you. Their original recipe calls for virgin olive oil and imported vodka, and, yes, it makes a difference. But they understand that I needed to make a few minor changes to their original, just to make it easier to make at home with readily available ingredients. So, what are you waiting for? If you can't take a trip to Chicago, here's a way to enjoy the tastes of Italy and Chicago in every bite.

Rosebud's Farfalle alla Vodka

4 to 6 servings

1 tablespoon olive oil
1 tablespoon chopped garlic
¼ cup vodka
1 can (28 ounces) whole tomatoes,
    undrained, coarsely chopped
1 package (12 ounces) bow tie
    pasta

1 container (8 ounces) mascarpone
    cheese
2 tablespoons coarsely chopped
    fresh basil
1 teaspoon salt
1 teaspoon black pepper

In a medium-sized saucepan, heat the olive oil over medium heat. Add the garlic and sauté for 1 to 2 minutes, just until browned. Add the vodka and the tomatoes with their juice and bring to a boil. Reduce the heat to low and simmer for 15 minutes. Meanwhile, prepare the pasta according to the package directions; drain, rinse, and drain again. Return the pasta to its cooking pot and cover to keep warm. Add the remaining ingredients to the tomato mixture and stir until thoroughly combined and the cheese is melted. Pour over the pasta and stir until combined, rewarming over low heat, if necessary. Serve immediately.

When I travel around the country, visiting my Mr. Food stations, I take a lot of "ribbing" from the TV anchors. We have a lot of fun kidding each other. I look forward to it. But another way I enjoy getting "ribbed" is at the dinner table.

Ever since the first time I went to the Country Tavern in Kilgore, Texas, every time I go to a new city, I ask the local folks where I can find the best ribs. Chinese-style pork ribs, Texas-style short ribs . . . I don't care. There are so many different ways to make them, and every city seems to give them its own twist. I love the taste of meat cooked on the bone, so the next time I'm visiting your city, please, please, come on and "rib me"!

Chinese Spareribs

4 to 6 servings

8 garlic cloves, minced
2 teaspoons salt
2 cans (10¼ ounces each)
    condensed beef broth
½ cup ketchup

½ cup honey
½ cup soy sauce
3 to 4 pounds pork spareribs,
    cut into individual ribs

In a 9"× 13" glass baking dish, combine the garlic and salt; mix well. Add the remaining ingredients except the spareribs and blend until well mixed. Add the ribs, turning to coat well. Cover and refrigerate for at least 4 hours, or overnight, turning occasionally. Preheat the oven to 450°F. Line a large roasting pan with aluminum foil and add ½ inch of water to the pan. Coat a roasting rack with nonstick vegetable spray and place it in the pan. Place the spareribs crosswise on the rack, reserving the marinade for basting. Roast for 10 minutes, then reduce the heat to 350°F. and roast for 1 hour and 20 minutes, or until the ribs are tender and the glaze is crispy, basting occasionally with the reserved marinade, **except during the last 10 minutes**. Discard any remaining marinade.

NOTE: Placing the ribs in a hot oven for the first 10 minutes gives them a nice crispy coating. If you're into spicy Chinese flavor, serve these with hot mustard.

Cola Ribs

4 to 5 servings

1 teaspoon garlic powder
1 teaspoon salt
1 teaspoon black pepper
4 to 5 pounds beef short ribs
3 tablespoons vegetable oil
1 can (12 ounces) carbonated cola
    beverage (not diet)

1 bottle (12 ounces) chili sauce
2 tablespoons Worcestershire sauce
2 tablespoons hot pepper sauce
1 teaspoon sugar

In a small bowl, combine the garlic powder, salt, and pepper. Rub the mixture over the ribs, completely covering them. In a large pot, heat the oil over medium-high heat and brown the ribs on all sides. Meanwhile, in a large bowl, combine the remaining ingredients. When the ribs are brown, drain the liquid from the pot; pour the cola mixture over the ribs, cover, and cook over medium heat for 1½ to 2 hours, or until tender, turning and basting the ribs occasionally with the cooking liquid.

NOTE: Serve with the pan drippings as a dipping sauce.

I enjoy getting "ribbed" at the dinner table.

East Coast, West Coast, and everywhere in between. . . . I'm always thrilled to make appearances and meet my fans. And whatever city I'm in, after I check out the ribs, I like to try the foods that are native to the area. For example, when I'm in Kansas City, Missouri, it's time to roll up my sleeves for down-home barbecue. I've sure had some great barbecue at Gates and Sons Restaurant and Arthur Bryant's Restaurant. Sure, it's a bit messy, but once you dig in, you're in for a treat.

In 1984, a group from my Kansas City station took me to a little place called Stroud's Restaurant. The piano player keeps the atmosphere upbeat and lively, but it's the panfried chicken and country-fried steak that really pack them in. I asked their cook for the secret of his steaks and he told me it's the "cracklings" left in the pan from the last time he cooked chicken. Mmm. . . .

Stroud's Chicken-Fried Steak

6 servings

1⅔ cups all-purpose flour, divided
1 tablespoon paprika
2 teaspoons salt, divided
1 teaspoon black pepper, divided
1 egg

4 cups milk, divided
6 beef cubed steaks
   (5 to 6 ounces each)
1 cup vegetable oil, divided

In a shallow dish, combine 1⅓ cups flour, the paprika, 1 teaspoon salt, and ½ teaspoon pepper. In another shallow dish, beat the egg with 1 cup milk. Dredge each steak thoroughly in the seasoned flour, then coat each with the milk mixture and again with the flour mixture. Heat 3 tablespoons oil in a large skillet over medium heat. Add 3 of the coated steaks and cook for 10 to 14 minutes, until golden on both sides, adding 3 tablespoons oil to the skillet and turning halfway through the cooking. Place the steaks on a platter and cover to keep warm. Repeat with the remaining steaks. Add the remaining ¼ cup oil to the skillet and heat over medium heat. Slowly stir in the remaining ⅓ cup flour until the consistency of paste. Bring to a boil over medium-high heat, then slowly add the remaining 3 cups milk, stirring constantly. Reduce the heat to medium and cook until the gravy comes to a boil, stirring constantly with a whisk or a spoon. Add the remaining 1 teaspoon salt and ½ teaspoon pepper; mix well. Serve the gravy over the cooked steaks.

L et's talk Chile—the country, not the pepper, although it was as hot as a pepper when we landed in Santiago on January 18, 1992. I was fortunate to be part of a group of food editors and others in the food industry who were treated to a well-planned trip to see all that the country's food producers have to offer. We were taken on a nonstop tour of plantations, packing houses, wineries. . . . Just look at these photos! The berry packers look more like surgeons than anyone would believe. And, oh, what food Chile produces! Plums, nectarines, peaches, raspberries, salmon, wines . . .

You've got to try this simple recipe for a favorite Chilean sweet called manjar. It's so versatile that it can be used as a dip, a fruit or ice cream sauce, or even a cake or phyllo dough filling. I bet you can come up with a few more of your own uses. Oh, what a time we had! It was as sweet as manjar.

PHOTOGRAPH COURTESY OF CARYL SAUNDERS ASSOCIATES

Manjar

1¾ cups

1 can (14 ounces) sweetened condensed milk

Preheat the oven to 350°F. Remove the top from the can and cover tightly with aluminum foil. Place the can in a 9" × 5" loaf pan and fill with boiling water to within 1 inch of the rim of the can. Cover the pan tightly with aluminum foil. Bake for 3 hours, or until the milk is caramel-colored. Holding the can with oven mitts, scrape the milk into a blender or food processor and blend until very creamy and smooth. Serve warm, or cover and chill until ready to serve.

NOTE: Serve this warm or cold as a dip for whole raspberries, blackberries, strawberries, or cut-up apples or other fruit.

Tell your office staff you're off to Jamaica on a business trip, and see how much sympathy you get. Don't get me wrong—I love seeing new places and touring food production facilities. But these trips are hard work. We're constantly on the go.

This trip landed me in Kingston, Jamaica, where, with the help of Israeli agricultural consultants, the farming is rich and the crops plentiful. The farming methods have been brought up to date and now there is one man working an average of 40 acres, rather than the old way of 40 men working one acre. The fish hatcheries produce amazing results. Their tilapia is among the finest I've had. It's a delicate white-fleshed fish . . . well, instead of telling you about it, here you can see a farmer holding one that's been plucked right out of the holding tanks.

Yes, my trip to Jamaica was very impressive. Anyone who didn't believe in the value of technology would have been converted after seeing what wonderful things are going on there.

An A student I wasn't, but I've always been curious—about almost everything! I'd say that I have a never-ending appetite for knowledge, especially about food. I read as much about it as I can get my hands on. And I try to pass on this thirst for knowledge to today's young people.

For a number of years I've been fortunate to work with the wonderful folks at Keebler on an educational video/hands-on cooking series. The program has been used successfully in high schools around the country to teach students how fun and easy it can be to prepare food for themselves and their families. So don't be surprised if you catch me or my Keebler program teaching you or your kids the art of "OOH IT'S SO GOOD!!"

Fresh from the Hollow Tree

COURTESY OF KEEBLER®

212

Give me a plastic tasting spoon and my ever-so-sharp pocket knife and off I go! Tasting, that is. As a national food celebrity, I've been asked to judge many food contests. Which onion is the sweetest? Which chicken wing is the hottest? Which chili has the most zing?

As a judge for the Kahlúa® Bake-Off, it was my job to taste 42 different desserts, each loaded with the coffee-flavored liqueur. After the first dozen or so, I think my taste buds were a bit tipsy. But, true professional that I am, I kept going and found this absolutely incredible cake. Then I let Ethel drive home.

Speaking of taste buds, the day I worked on the McIlhenny Tabasco® Sauce Cook-off, mine were more alive than they've ever been (before or since)! Boy, that's powerful stuff! So here I've got not the contest-winning recipe, but, rather, Walter McIlhenny's own famous chunky chili. It's definitely got a kick. But, after all, isn't that what chili's all about?!

Kahlúa® Mexican Chocolate Cake

10 to 12 servings

1 package (18.25 ounces)
   devil's food cake mix
3 eggs
1½ cups plus 2 tablespoons
   Kahlúa®, divided
½ cup vegetable oil

1½ teaspoons ground cinnamon,
   divided
1 container (16 ounces)
   chocolate frosting
¼ teaspoon unsweetened cocoa

Preheat the oven to 350°F. In a large bowl, with an electric beater on low speed, beat the cake mix, eggs, 1½ cups Kahlúa®, the oil, and 1 teaspoon cinnamon until the cake mix is moistened. Increase the speed to medium and beat for 2 more minutes, or until smooth. Pour the batter into two 8-inch cake pans that have been lightly greased and floured. Bake for 30 to 35 minutes, until a wooden toothpick inserted in the center comes out clean. Let cool in the pans for 10 minutes, then remove to a wire rack to cool completely. In a small bowl, combine the frosting and the remaining 2 tablespoons Kahlúa® and ½ teaspoon cinnamon; mix well. Fill and frost the cooled layers, then sprinkle the top with the cocoa. Serve immediately, or cover loosely and chill until ready to use.

Mr. McIlhenny's Chili

4 to 6 servings

¼ cup vegetable oil
3 pounds lean boneless beef chuck
    roast, well trimmed and
    cut into 1-inch cubes
1 medium-sized onion, chopped
3 garlic cloves, minced
3 tablespoons chili powder

2 teaspoons ground cumin
2 teaspoons salt
2 teaspoons Tabasco® pepper sauce
3 cups water
1 can (4.5 ounces) chopped
    green chilies, drained

In a large saucepan, heat the oil over medium-high heat; add the beef and cook for 5 minutes. Drain off the liquid. Add the onion and garlic and sauté for 5 minutes, stirring frequently, until the beef is browned on all sides and the onion is tender. Add the chili powder, cumin, salt, and pepper sauce; stir and cook for 1 minute. Add the water and chilies and bring to a boil, stirring occasionally. Reduce the heat to low, cover, and simmer for 45 minutes, stirring occasionally. Remove the lid and simmer for 45 more minutes, or until the beef is fork-tender, stirring occasionally.

NOTE: Serve over rice and garnish with chopped onions, shredded cheese, and sour cream, if desired.

Traveling in my early days as Mr. Food, I would often be met at the airport by an intern from the local television station. Many of the young interns weren't familiar with Mr. Food, so they didn't know what I looked like. The promotion or news director would tell them to look for a stocky man with a beard, maybe with a hat, and carrying a big bag. From that description, they probably expected to greet Santa at the curb, not Mr. Food! Oh, well, I can hope to be as recognized as that other famous character!

Reindeer Cookies

about 5 dozen cookies

½ cup (1 stick) butter, softened
¼ cup light molasses
¼ cup dark molasses
½ cup sugar
1 tablespoon white vinegar

2 cups all-purpose flour
1 teaspoon ground cinnamon
½ teaspoon ground ginger
1½ teaspoons baking soda

In a small saucepan, combine the butter, light and dark molasses, sugar, and vinegar. Bring to a boil over medium heat and boil gently for 3 minutes, stirring constantly. Remove from the heat and allow to cool. In a medium-sized bowl, combine the remaining ingredients; slowly add the cooled molasses mixture, stirring constantly until smooth. Shape the dough into 2 balls, wrap each in waxed paper, and chill for several hours, or overnight. Preheat the oven to 375°F. On a lightly floured surface, roll out the dough to a ⅛-inch thickness. Cut out cookies with a 2-inch round cookie cutter, or use a reindeer cutter, and place 2 inches apart on cookie sheets that have been coated with nonstick baking spray. Bake for 7 to 8 minutes, or until the cookies are a rich brown color. Immediately remove from the cookie sheets and allow to cool on wire racks.

NOTE: These cookies aren't just for Santa and his reindeer—I've known many a boy and girl to eat them up (moms and dads, too)!

219

Talk about mistaken identities . . . ! For years our mail has been full of photos of people who swear they're Mr. Food look-alikes. Here are a few. What do you think? There's even little David Muscatello, from South Lake, Texas, dressed up for Halloween . . . as Mr. Food! His mom said his costume made a big hit.

They say that imitation is the sincerest form of flattery, and I am flattered by all the attention. I especially love it when my grandchildren get into the act, too. Here's my oldest, Shayna, having ice cream with her friend "Chef" Michael Pepe. They get such a kick out of themselves!

Oh, and here's a bunch of us taking a minute out during a recent show taping to wish our dear friend up north, Michael Cocca, a happy birthday on tape.

Once again I greeted Ethel with the exciting news of a Mr. Food agricultural tour. This time I was invited to visit Israel and I was allowed to take her with me. We had our bags packed in no time, 'cause we'd wanted to take a trip like this for years. We knew it was going to be special in so many ways.

From the moment we touched down at Tel Aviv International Airport every moment was magical. Each farm, or *kibbutz*, as the Israelis call them, street vendor, and winding street that we encountered offered us a variety of unforgettable experiences.

Oh, those Israeli breakfasts! The offerings of cheeses, fish, fruits, and salads were endless. What a way to start off a long day of touring! On the next page you can see me viewing the latest techniques for growing hothouse cherry tomatoes. Israelis sure do know how to surmount obstacles. We were amazed as we were shown the numerous ways that Israel's farmers make the most of unfavorable growing conditions.

Before we left, Ethel and I visited with our Israeli friends, Ceil and Buna. Each of them made sure we experienced different aspects of Israeli life and its rich religious history. We stood at the Western Wall, shaking as we thought about the years that had passed and the events that had taken place on the land beneath our feet. There, on that land holy to people of so many of the world's religions, our tears of awe turned to ones of appreciation as we left with a renewed sense of what is possible.

Israeli Chopped Salad

6 to 8 servings (about ½ cup dressing)

2 medium-sized cucumbers,
    peeled, seeded, and diced
2 medium-sized green bell peppers,
    diced
3 medium-sized tomatoes, seeded
    and diced
¼ cup chopped onion
1 can (2¼ ounces) sliced black
    olives, drained
1 can (15 to 19 ounces) garbanzo
    beans (chick peas), rinsed
    and drained

DRESSING
⅓ cup olive oil
3 tablespoons lemon juice
½ teaspoon white pepper
1½ teaspoons salt
4 teaspoons white vinegar

In a large bowl, combine the cucumbers, green peppers, tomatoes, onion, olives, and garbanzo beans. In a small bowl, combine the dressing ingredients; mix well. Pour the dressing over the vegetables and stir to coat. Cover and chill for 2 to 3 hours, or overnight, allowing the mixture to marinate before serving.

NOTE: If you can, make this a day in advance so that the flavors have more time to "marry."

Just mention New York City and most people think of the Statue of Liberty, the Empire State Building, the excitement of Times Square, and the noisy traffic. Then there's the food . . . oh, the food. In New York City, you can get any kind of food you want. And no trip to New York is complete for me without a trip to Sammy's Famous Roumanian Steak House and the grandfather of all New York delis, the Carnegie Delicatessen and Restaurant.

Sammy's is a small place on the Lower East Side. The food is like none you'll find anywhere else, except maybe in Grandma's kitchen. And that's perfect, since everyone is treated like family at Sammy's. They put the old-style seltzer bottle, the carton of milk, and the chocolate syrup right on your table so you can mix your own egg creams. They mix the chopped liver at your table—and leave you with a container of chicken fat so you can add as much as you want. The steaks, chops, and potatoes are packed with flavor. And the frozen vodka . . . well, it's a good thing you can get home by taxi!

Delicatessens around the country often try to copy the magic of the Carnegie in midtown Manhattan, but it's a place you've got to experience firsthand. And you'd better bring a load of hungry friends with you because the size of the portions, especially the overstuffed sandwiches, is not to be believed! Check out this one—even I had a hard time taking the first bite! After filling up on the warming chicken soup, the corned beef, pastrami, coleslaw, pickles, and potato pancakes, you've got to try one of their fabulous desserts. (I'm partial to the cheesecake.)

Ready for a field trip to New York's restaurants now? This is just the beginning! There are so many wonderful places there to eat that you can be sure you'll never leave New York hungry!

If you ever accompanied me to Philadelphia, you can bet we'd stop at Pat's King of Steaks, where the Philadelphia cheese steak sandwich was born. Pat's is in a small wedge-shaped building in South Philly. I'd order you up a sandwich covered in cheese and piled with toppings, and we'd sit at one of the outdoor tables so we could enjoy the sights, sounds, and smells of South Philly.

Philadelphia Cheese Steak Sandwiches

4 sandwiches

3 tablespoons vegetable oil
2 large onions, thinly sliced
1 to 1¼ pounds thinly sliced roast beef
½ teaspoon salt

¼ teaspoon black pepper
4 hoagie or hero rolls, split
4 slices (1 ounce each) provolone cheese

Preheat the oven to 350°F. In a large skillet, heat the oil over medium-high heat. Add the onions and sauté for 5 to 7 minutes, or until tender and lightly browned. Add the roast beef, salt, and pepper. Sauté for 3 to 4 minutes, or until the beef is completely heated through. Use tongs to divide the meat mixture evenly among the roll bottoms. Place the open sandwiches on a large cookie sheet and place a slice of cheese over each. Bake for 3 to 4 minutes, or until the cheese has melted. Cover with the tops of the rolls and serve immediately.

My trips to Philadelphia have become much more frequent since 1993. That was the year I was lucky enough to meet the team at QVC, now the largest home shopping network. They stand for Quality, Value, and Convenience and, boy, what an operation they've got!

I'll never forget my first QVC appearance. It was just host Jane Rudolph Treacy and me . . . and millions of viewers! I was demonstrating recipes from my most recent cookbook and chatting with a phone caller when the producer started motioning to us to wrap it up. It was kind of like when bad vaudeville acts were dragged off the stage with cane hooks! What I didn't know was that absolutely

nothing was wrong. In fact, everything was right! We had sold out of my books and the phone lines were jammed. On that first appearance, we sold 8,000 books in just 12 minutes! And, since then, I've returned to QVC on a regular basis to share the kitchen with a number of wonderful hosts and to introduce each new set of Mr. Food cookbooks to their fabulously receptive audience.

Last winter I got a special QVC treat—I did several live shows with Bob Bowersox via remote from Key West, Florida. Check out my straw hat! I just had to have it for those spots, then for the QVC cruise that followed, where I did hands-on demonstrations as we traveled through the Caribbean and the Panama Canal.

I did hands-on demonstrations. . . .

Here I am sharing kitchen secrets in Bob's segment, *In the Kitchen with Bob*. Off the air, Bob even shared one of his favorite recipes with me, which he included in his own cookbook. He told me that these crab cakes are the real thing—created by his mother-in-law, who is now 85 and still going strong. She's a traditional Polish cook who measures everything with her hands, never with a measuring cup or spoon. These are some of the best crab cakes I've ever tasted. Bob told me that he had to promise her to cut her grass for an entire summer just so she'd agree to give him her recipe. Bob went on to say, "Since that day I've enjoyed them at my house so many times . . . I'm sure it was worth all that lawn mowing!" I agree!

Granny's Crab Cakes

about 1½ dozen cakes

2 medium-sized carrots, peeled and cut into chunks
1 medium-sized green bell pepper, cut into chunks
1 medium-sized onion, cut into chunks
1 tablespoon butter
1 pound crabmeat or imitation crabmeat, shredded

2 eggs
½ teaspoon salt
⅛ teaspoon black pepper
1 package (8 ounces) dry herb-seasoned stuffing
1 cup plain dry bread crumbs
½ to 1 cup vegetable oil

In a blender or a food processor that has been fitted with its metal cutting blade, process the carrots, bell pepper, and onion until finely chopped. In a large skillet, melt the butter over medium-low heat and sauté the chopped vegetables until heated through; set aside to cool in the skillet. When cooled, transfer to a large bowl and add the crabmeat, eggs, salt, and black pepper; mix well. Add the dry stuffing; mix thoroughly. Place the bread crumbs in a shallow dish. Form about 18 equal-sized patties, using about ⅓ cup of the mixture for each patty. Completely coat the patties in the bread crumbs. In the skillet, heat 2 tablespoons oil over medium-low heat and sauté the crab cakes, a few at a time, for 6 to 8 minutes, or until lightly browned, turning halfway through the cooking and adding more oil as needed. Drain on paper towels and serve immediately.

RECIPE COURTESY OF BOB BOWERSOX

A cruise ship sure is different from my navy one! No more uniform—for me, anyway. All of our cruise ship captains have been extremely hospitable, and they sure look a lot better than I did in my work uniform! Oh, and the cruise food . . . it's definitely spectacular. If the navy had been anything like this, I might have made it a career!

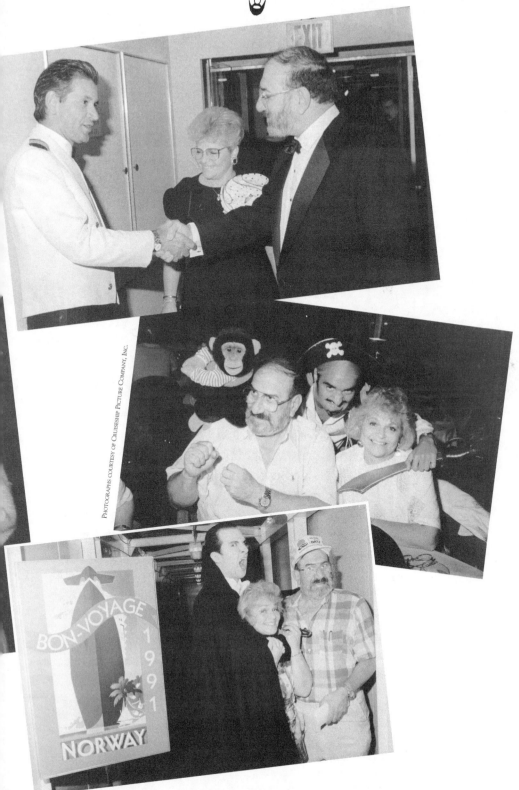

I've met so many great people, but I could definitely say that I could have lived without crossing the paths of Bob and Andrew . . . the hurricanes, I mean. When Bob slammed the Northeast, Ethel and I were spending some time in Rhode Island. Chuck and his wife, Tammy, were visiting us there, and we all ended up staying in a hurricane shelter for a few days, with me doing on-site storm updates for Providence's WJAR–TV and Miami's WPLG–TV via cellular phone. There were hundreds of people stranded at the shelter, and that is where we met Roy and Deloris Simpson. This was the start of a wonderful friendship with 2 special people who'd joined us in helping to feed the people stuck in the shelter.

That would have been more than enough firsthand hurricane knowledge for us, but, no! Andrew ripped across South Florida in 1994, and, fortunately for us, spared us and our home. But we were there to lend a hand to those who needed help in the storm's aftermath.

I've recently begun reporting for my storm-prone stations with safety tips and ideas about what foods and related items to have on hand for emergencies. Some good planning can be a life-saver.

After experiencing a hurricane, or any other life-threatening situation, people often step back and reevaluate their values and priorities. I feel so fortunate to have a healthy family, to have always had food on our table, and to work at something that is so challenging, rewarding, and enjoyable. My dad always taught us to share with those less fortunate, even when we didn't have much ourselves. He'd be proud of our family's success, but he'd be even prouder of what we're giving back to the community.

The entire Mr. Food team brainstormed and did our homework to find an organization that we could team up with to share our good fortune. We found out about Second Harvest®, a national organization that, by way of local chapters, gathers excess food from manufacturers and various other sources, then distributes it to the needy. The folks at Second Harvest® were more than happy to have us on their team. I've done public service announcements for distribution to Mr. Food stations around the country to help get the word out about Second Harvest®'s good work. And I feel so strongly about what they and others like them do that I've dedicated this book to their efforts.

Here's Christine Vladimiroff, OSB, President of Second Harvest®, taking part in the disaster relief program after Hurricane Andrew destroyed whole communities in South Florida in 1992. Christine was kind enough to share one of her special family recipes with us.

PHOTOGRAPH COURTESY OF SECOND HARVEST®

Christine's Angelic Shrimp and Pasta

6 to 8 servings

1 package (16 ounces) angel
  hair pasta
1 pound large shrimp, peeled and
  deveined, with tails left on
⅔ cup olive oil
⅓ cup sun-dried tomatoes
  packed in oil, chopped

3 garlic cloves, crushed
2 tablespoons chopped fresh basil
½ teaspoon salt
¼ teaspoon crushed red pepper
¼ teaspoon black pepper
¼ cup grated Parmesan cheese

Cook the pasta according to the package directions. Drain, rinse, and drain again; set aside in a large bowl. Rinse the shrimp and pat dry. In a large skillet, heat the oil over medium heat and add the shrimp, sun-dried tomatoes, garlic, basil, salt, and red and black peppers. Cook for 3 to 4 minutes, turning the shrimp to cook on all sides. Add to the pasta and sprinkle with the Parmesan cheese; toss well and serve immediately.

It's normal to hear my son Steve picking up the phone and booking camera crews for on-location tapings. And boy, was one crew thrilled to find out that this particular taping was to be done at the Atlantis Resort on Paradise Island! Okay, the location was paradise, but it was still work. That's why I needed Ethel to take care of me and to powder my face (since most of our taping was done outside, in the beautiful, intense sunshine), Howard to assist in the abundant food preparation, and his wife, Patty, to assist with the props. What a team!

We had a little time to appreciate the island and its wonderful fresh fish and other food while we were there. This marinade is one of our favorite tasty memories, and we're glad we can make it at home for our grilled chicken and fish.

Want to know the hardest part of that whole taping? Keeping our frozen piña colada props from melting before we finished taping each shot!

Caribbean Citrus Marinade

Enough for 2 pounds fish or chicken fillets

½ of a medium-sized onion,
   cut into chunks
3 garlic cloves, peeled
2 tablespoons olive oil
Juice of 1 medium-sized lemon

Juice of 1 medium-sized lime
Juice of 1 medium-sized orange
2 drops hot pepper sauce
¼ teaspoon ground allspice
½ teaspoon salt

Place all the ingredients in a blender or a food processor that has been fitted with its metal cutting blade and process for 1 minute, or until well combined. Use immediately as directed in the Note.

NOTE: After blending the marinade, pour it into a glass baking dish and add white-fleshed fish or chicken fillets. Cover and chill for at least 4 hours, or overnight, turning occasionally. Remove the fillets from the marinade, discarding the excess marinade, and cook the fillets on a preheated medium-high grill or in the oven at 350°F.

When people around the country hear "Buffalo, New York," they usually think of a place known for its cold, snowy winters and the city that gave us hot Buffalo chicken wings. Buffalo's one of my favorite towns, and I can tell you, the famous wings really were born there, at a place called Frank and Teressa's Anchor Bar & Restaurant.

It was late one Friday night in 1964 when Teressa Bellissimo needed something quick to serve to her son's hungry friends. She'd been about to drop a batch of chicken wings into a stockpot to make soup, but she decided to do something else with them instead. At first, her son, "The Rooster," and his friends were surprised by what she'd whipped up, but after they tasted

her creation, their fate was sealed. Oh, don't forget that real Buffalo wings are served with celery sticks and blue cheese dressing. And now they're served at Duff's, LaNova, Mammoser's, and lots of other wing places around Buffalo and the rest of the country, too. In fact, there are a number of places outside of Buffalo, like the Quaker Steak and Lube in Sharon, Pennsylvania, that swear that their wings are the best.

So who really makes the best chicken wings? Choose your own favorites . . . I like 'em all!

Home of the ...
Original Buffalo Chicken Wings

Q Who did John Wayne play in True Grit?
A Rooster Cogburn.

Wings

Did you know ....
Visiting teams that come to Buffalo visit the Anchor Bar the night before the game.

You can always Wing it with famous Chicken Wings celery sticks & bleu cheese

Any way you want them - plain, mild, medium, hot or su (if you're daring!)

Single (10)......................
Double (20)......................
Bucket (50)......................
Extra celery sticks or hot sau
Extra bleu cheese dressing .

COURTESY OF FRANK AND TERESSA'S ANCHOR BAR & RESTAURANT, BUFF

Flavorful chicken wings, celery sticks, and blue cheese dressing. . . . Imagine creating such an unusual, yummy combination! Thanks, Teressa!

Buffalo Wings

40 to 50 wings

10 pounds chicken wings (thawed if frozen)

1 cup (2 sticks) butter
1½ cups cayenne pepper sauce

Preheat the oven to 425°F. Split the wings at each joint and discard the tips; rinse, then pat dry. Place the wings on cookie sheets and bake for 30 minutes. Turn the wings and bake for an additional 30 minutes, until browned. Drain well and place in a large bowl. In a small saucepan, melt the butter over medium-low heat. Turn off the heat and stir in the hot pepper sauce; toss with the cooked chicken wings. Serve warm.

NOTE: You can bake the wings ahead of time and store them in the fridge or freezer; then, before serving, simply warm them in the oven and toss them with the sauce.

You know where you can find me every year on the first weekend in March—in Buffalo, New York, at the annual Variety Club Telethon. It's indescribable how all of western New York comes together for this event.

Everyone rolls up his or her sleeves to raise money for the Children's Hospital. What great people! What big hearts! And I'm honored to be a part of it all. Thank *you*, Variety Club, WKBW–TV, and volunteers for making this event so successful year after year. Thank you for including me. We *do* make a difference.

Bon voyage . . . again! QVC's Caribbean cruise wasn't the only one where I donned my hat, apron, and sunscreen. Ethel and I hosted an Alaskan cruise sponsored by WKBW–TV of Buffalo, New York. And, by the way, the cruise ship wasn't our only transportation during those 2 weeks. And it wasn't our only view of the beautiful Alaskan landscape, either. No, sir—we sought even more exhilaration (don't ask me why!), so we got into the necessary gear and went white-water rafting! I had a feeling nobody would believe we did it, so here's the picture to prove it!

Fortunately, we spent the evenings relaxing and getting to know the wonderful WKBW group. Together, we enjoyed the fresh-caught native salmon and unwound while taking in the beauty of the glaciers. We all agreed that it was Mother Nature's way of saying, "Ooh it's so beautiful . . . and tasty!"

Salmon in Creamy Dill Sauce

4 servings

2 tablespoons butter
¾ cup half-and-half
¼ cup dry white wine
1 tablespoon lemon juice

1 tablespoon chopped
  fresh dillweed
Four 4-ounce salmon fillets,
  skin removed

In a large skillet, melt the butter over medium-high heat. Add the remaining ingredients except the salmon; stir well. Add the salmon and reduce the heat to medium-low. Simmer for 12 to 15 minutes, or until the fish flakes easily with a fork, turning halfway through the cooking. Place the salmon on a serving platter and serve topped with the sauce.

PHOTOGRAPHS COURTESY OF WKBW-TV, BUFFALO, N.Y.

Meeting people . . . making new friends . . . that's what I love about this business! I enjoy meeting fans and associates, too. For example, when I was at the annual NATPE (National Association of Television Producers and Executives—see, that's why I used the letters!) convention in Las Vegas, I had a chance to get together with my King World family. Here I am with Nancy Glass, host of *American Journal,* and, you know—or do you need to buy a vowel?—*Wheel of Fortune*'s Vanna White. While Vanna was checking out some of *my* easy recipes, Nancy was telling me about one of her own easy favorites. It's family-sized cheese puffs that she gladly agreed to let me share with you.

Family-Sized Cheese Puffs

6 to 8 servings

1 package (8 ounces) refrigerated
  crescent roll dough
Two 7-ounce Gouda cheese
  rounds, rinds removed

1 egg, lightly beaten

Preheat the oven to 350°F. Unroll the dough on a clean work surface. Divide it along the center perforation into two 7" × 8" rectangles. Pinch together the perforations on each half and place a cheese round in the center of each. Wrap the cheese by stretching the dough up and around the cheese; pinch to close completely. Place seam side down on a large rimmed baking sheet that has been coated with nonstick vegetable spray and brush the dough with the beaten egg. Bake for 15 to 18 minutes, until the tops are golden. Place the whole puffs on a platter and let your gang cut them into wedges.

Thanks, Nancy, for sharing
your easy family favorite!

I think I'll let Rolonda Watts of *Rolonda* speak for herself with her letter and recipe. I love you, too, Rolonda—and *I'm* always honored to share my kitchen with *you!*

Dear Mr. Food,

You know I love you and have most all of your scrumptious cookbooks! But I must tell you, I am simply honored to now have a chance to share with you and your readers a morsel or two of my own home-cooking recipes. Thank you . . . and now . . . from my kitchen to yours. . . .

Being a real worker bee, I rarely ever get a chance to really completely settle down and do something as simple and wonderful as fussing over a well-simmered stew. Whenever I do go all out with cooking . . . it is really my way of going all out for my family and friends. Cooking my favorite dishes for them is my way of saying, "I truly love you." What are still my favorite recipes from down home in North Carolina are now favorites among my friends. Perhaps your readers will make them their favorites, too. After all, a good home-cooked meal is like the difference between a long-distance phone call and a hug at the door. It's that warm feeling of home . . . and that's mighty special!

Enjoy and good luck!

Rolonda

Rolonda's Easy Spicy Corn Bread

12 to 15 servings

2 packages (8½ ounces each)
   corn muffin mix
2 tablespoons vegetable oil
4 jalapeño peppers, chopped
   (2 tablespoons)

½ cup corn kernels
1 tablespoon sour cream
2 teaspoons honey

Preheat the oven to 400°F. Prepare the corn muffin mix according to the package directions. Place the batter in a large bowl and add the remaining ingredients; mix well. Pour into a greased 9" × 13" baking dish and bake for 10 to 12 minutes, until golden. Let cool, then slice and serve.

NOTE: Rolonda says she likes to sprinkle a little paprika on top for nice color, and she serves it with butter.

During the planning of this book, Caryl, Howard, and I agreed that our editor, Zachary Schisgal, should be represented with a recipe of his own for a change. We asked him, and he was a bit apprehensive, since he's a single guy living in New York City—where almost any type of food you'd ever want can easily be "taken out." Zach admits that that's usually the easiest thing to do at the end of his hectic workdays. That may be true, but if Zach had an occasion to invite people over for his version of a home-cooked meal, it would most likely feature this throw-together dish that tastes like so much more. Okay, Zach, if cooking makes you that uncomfortable, then I'll let *you* stick to the editing while *I* do the cooking!

Easy Chicken Divine

4 servings

1 tablespoon olive oil
4 boneless, skinless chicken breast
    halves (2 pounds total)
¼ teaspoon salt
¼ teaspoon black pepper
1 package (10 ounces) frozen
    broccoli florets, thawed and
    drained

1 can (10¾ ounces) condensed
    cream of chicken soup
1 cup (4 ounces) shredded
    Cheddar cheese

Preheat the oven to 375°F. In a large skillet, heat the olive oil over medium-high heat. Season the chicken with the salt and pepper. Sauté the chicken in the hot oil for 10 minutes, or until browned, turning halfway through the cooking. Meanwhile, place the broccoli florets in the bottom of a 7" × 11" baking dish that has been coated with nonstick vegetable spray. Place the browned chicken on the broccoli, then pour the soup over the chicken. Sprinkle with the cheese and bake for 30 minutes, or until no pink remains in the chicken and the cheese is golden.

From my days spent playing in the tomato and corn fields of Upstate New York to today, when I tape Mr. Food shows from every growing field I can, I've loved being out there with the fresh fruits and veggies. I talk to local farmers and major agricultural producers, too, to get their impressions and learn about new advances and trends.

I wish you could see these photos in full color, because the Salad Savoy in these fields is every shade of green and purple that you could imagine. It's becoming a popular addition to salads and stir-fries lately, though it's still great for its former primary use—as a fresh, colorful, edible garnish. How versatile can a vegetable be!

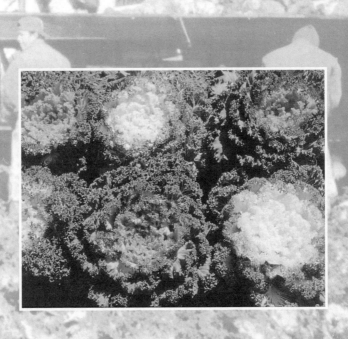

Writing this book has given me the perfect opportunity to relive so many wonderful times spent with my mom, dad, and Flo; my partner in life, Ethel; my three wonderful children, Steve, Caryl, and Chuck; and my friends, fans, and business associates. But my real pride is now focused on my grandchildren, who all live just a short drive from our home.

Here's our oldest, Shayna, our twins, Jessie and Beth, and our first grandson, Sam. And by the time this book is published, Caryl and Roy will have provided Shayna with a much-awaited brother or sister, and Chuck and Tammy will be welcoming a new sibling for Sam. Steve and his wife, Carol (notice she spells her name C-a-r-O-l, as opposed to our daughter, C-a-r-Y-l—yes, it does get confusing!), have assured us that their two girls are more than enough to round out their family. Oh, do these children love each other! You should see them when they're all together. And you should see Ethel and *me* when they're all together! We're the beaming Grandma and Pop-Pop (that's what they call me).

As I watch the young ones play, learn, and grow, I think about how lucky I am. I often think of my friend Tevye, longing for a life of material and spiritual wealth as he sings "If I Were a Rich Man" in *Fiddler on the Roof*. I know I am rich— rich in family, good health, and lasting friendships.

May every person be as fortunate as I am, to open his eyes every morning and know a life full of

"OOH IT'S SO GOOD!!®"

Index

A

B

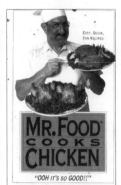

C

D

E

F

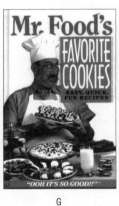

G

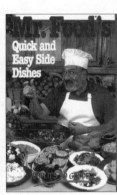

H

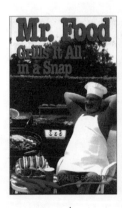

I

J

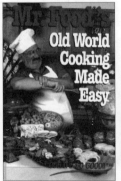

K

L

Mr. Food®'s Library Gives You More Ways to Say... "OOH IT'S SO GOOD!!®"

WILLIAM MORROW

M

N

O

P

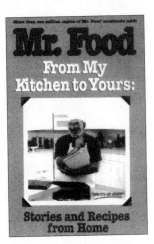

Q

Mr. Food®

Can Help You Be A Kitchen Hero!

Let Mr. Food® make your life easier with
Quick, No-Fuss Recipes and Helpful Kitchen Tips for

Family Dinners • Soups and Salads • Potluck Dishes
Barbecues • Special Brunches • Unbelievable Desserts

. . . and that's just the beginning!

Complete your Mr. Food® cookbook library today.
It's so simple to share in all the
"OOH IT'S SO GOOD!!®"

✂ -

TITLE	PRICE	QUANTITY	
A. Mr. Food® Cooks Like Mama	@ $12.95 each	x _____	= $_____
B. The Mr. Food® Cookbook, OOH IT'S SO GOOD!!®	@ $12.95 each	x _____	= $_____
C. Mr. Food® Cooks Chicken	@ $ 9.95 each	x _____	= $_____
D. Mr. Food® Cooks Pasta	@ $ 9.95 each	x _____	= $_____
E. Mr. Food® Makes Dessert	@ $ 9.95 each	x _____	= $_____
F. Mr. Food® Cooks Real American	@ $14.95 each	x _____	= $_____
G. Mr. Food®'s Favorite Cookies	@ $11.95 each	x _____	= $_____
H. Mr. Food®'s Quick and Easy Side Dishes	@ $11.95 each	x _____	= $_____
I. Mr. Food® Grills It All in a Snap	@ $11.95 each	x _____	= $_____
J. Mr. Food®'s Fun Kitchen Tips and Shortcuts (and Recipes, Too!)	@ $11.95 each	x _____	= $_____
K. Mr. Food®'s Old World Cooking Made Easy	@ $14.95 each	x _____	= $_____
L. "Help, Mr. Food®! Company's Coming!"	@ $14.95 each	x _____	= $_____
M. Mr. Food® Pizza 1-2-3	@ $12.00 each	x _____	= $_____
N. Mr. Food® Meat Around the Table	@ $12.00 each	x _____	= $_____
O. Mr. Food® Simply Chocolate	@ $12.00 each	x _____	= $_____
P. Mr. Food® A Little Lighter	@ $14.95 each	x _____	= $_____
Q. Mr. Food® From My Kitchen to Yours: Stories and Recipes from Home	@ $14.95 each	x _____	= $_____

Call 1-800-619-FOOD (3663) or send payment to:
Mr. Food®
P.O. Box 696
Holmes, PA 19043

Name _____

Street _____ Apt._____

City _____ State_____ Zip_____

Method of Payment: ☐ Check or Money Order Enclosed

☐ Credit Card: ☐ Visa ☐ MasterCard Expiration Date _____

Signature _____

Book Total	$_____
+$2.95 Postage & Handling First Copy *AND* $1 Ea. Add'l. Copy (Canadian Orders Add Add'l. $2.00 *Per Copy*)	$_____
Subtotal	$_____
Less $1.00 per book if ordering 3 or more books with this order	$ –_____
Add Applicable Sales Tax (FL Residents Only)	$_____
Total in U.S. Funds	$_____

Account #: ☐ ☐ ☐ ☐ ☐ ☐ ☐ ☐ ☐ ☐ ☐ ☐ ☐ ☐ ☐ ☐

Please allow 4 to 6 weeks for delivery.

BKQ1